Bedtime

Blessings

Volume 2

100 Bedtime Stories & Activities
for Blessing Your Child

Bedtime
Blessings
volume 2

100 Bedtime Stories & Activities
for Blessing Your Child

by
JOHN TRENT, Ph.D.

Tyndale House Publishers, Wheaton, Illinois

Heritage Builders

MORE BEDTIME BLESSINGS

Table of Contents

Introduction 1
The Blessings Box 3

Let's Play a Game: Treasure Hunt 5
Let's Sing a Song: Rock My Soul 6
Let's Make Something: Soap Cross 8
Let's Tell a Story: Alphabet Tales 10
Let's Play a Game: Tongue Twisters 12
Let's Talk About Feelings: Fear 14
Let's Play a Game: Story Cards 16
Let's Play a Game: Tic-Tac-Toe 18
Let's Do an Experiment: Penny Bath 20
Let's Play a Game: I Spy 22
Let's Learn Something: What's in a Name 24
Let's Learn Something: The Power to Hurt 26
Let's Do an Experiment: Invisible Ink 28
Let's Solve a Problem: The Envelope Puzzle 30
Let's Sing a Song: A New Tune 31
Let's Be Thankful: Our Wonderful Bodies 32
Let's Do an Experiment: Balancing Act 34
Let's Look in the Bible: Burning Words 36
Let's Learn Something: How to Whistle 38
Let's Play a Game: X Marks the Spot 40
Let's Talk About When I Was Your Age:
    Sharing Together 42
Let's Plant a Seed: Controlling Our Words 44

Let's Play a Game: Guess What? 46

Let's Take a Close Look: The Penny 48

Let's Make Up a Story: In the Picture 50

Let's Draw a Picture: A Wild Animal 52

Let's Talk About the Day: Bedtime Quiz 54

Let's Play a Game: Right on Target 56

Let's Write a Letter: With Love From... 58

Let's Hear a Story: The Lion and the Mouse 60

Let's Pray for Someone: A Friend with
  Special Needs 62

Let's Imagine: Drawing Mind Pictures 64

Let's Pretend: Crazy Questions 66

Let's Make a Wish: Learning to Be Thankful 68

Let's Talk About God: Three in One 70

Let's Look at Nature: How Do Plants Eat? 72

Let's Talk About the Future: The King Is Coming . . .74

Let's Read Together: Comic Book Cuddle 76

Let's Look in the Bible: Finding Answers 77

Let's Pretend: If Animals Could Talk 78

Let's Have a Riddle: Quick Riddles 80

Let's Write a Letter: With Thanks 82

Let's Play a Thinking Game: Clues 84

Let's Play a Game: Funny Bunny 86

Let's Play a Game: Squiggles 88

Let's Sing: Row Your Boat .90

Let's Write Something: Rhyme Time 92

Let's Look at Nature: Our Colorful Sun 94

Let's Play a Game: Rock, Scissors, Paper 96

Let's Play a Game: Memory Challenge 98
Let's Look at Nature: Butterfly Lessons 100
Let's Play a Game: Concentration 102
Let's Make Something: A Ceiling of Stars 104
Let's Think About Something: Our Generous God . .106
Let's Play a Game: Balloon Volleyball 108
Let's Read a Story: David and Goliath 110
Let's Talk About the Day: Good, Bad, or
    In-Between? 112
Let's Look in the Bible: Interruptions 114
Let's Plant a Seed: The Golden Rule 116
Let's Play a Game: Slapjack 118
Let's Build Something: House of Cards 120
Let's Talk About the Day: Things We Say 122
Let's Do a Few Riddles: Fast and Fun Ones 124
Let's Be Thankful: Rubber Band Reminders 126
Let's Talk Together: Our Day of Thanksgiving 128
Let's Play a Game: Helpful Hints 130
Let's Pretend: Fist Puppets 132
Let's Play a Game: Beddy-bye 134
Let's Talk About the Day: What If... 136
Let's Talk About the Day: Happy or Sad? 138
Let's Learn Something: The Redwood Tree 140
Let's Play a Game: Checkers 142
Let's Make Some Lists: All About You and Me 144
Let's Play a Game: Thumb Wrestling 146
Let's Sing a Song: Oh, How I Love Jesus 148
Let's Do Something Fun: Banana Bash 150

Let's Play a Game: Lightning Rounds 152
Let's Plan a Project: Cookie Choices 154
Let's Make Something: Cookies! 156
Let's Talk About Something: Hurting Words 158
Let's Make Something: Favorite Things Poster 160
Let's Talk Together: Your Favorite Things and You . .162
Let's Be Thankful: Thank You for Parents 163
Let's Do Something: Mailing You to
    Someone Special 164
Let's Find Out: "Why?" Questions 166
Let's Read a Book: Classic Stories 168
Let's Pretend: If I Were an Animal 170
Let's Write a Poem: Name Acrostic 173
Let's Look in the Bible: What Is Love? 174
Let's Talk About Choices: What Would You Do? . . .176
Let's Play a Game: Nim 178
Let's Look in the Bible: New Rules 180
Let's Look in the Bible: The Ten Commandments . . .182
Let's Play a Game: Non-stop Talk 184
Let's Read: Your Story 186
Let's Talk About Nature: Clouds 188
Let's Have a Riddle: Can You Guess? 190
Let's Pretend: Touched by Jesus 192
Let's Learn a New Word: Heaven 194
Let's Sing a Song: "Michael, Row the Boat Ashore" . . .196

Answer Page 198

Introduction

I feel strongly that there are moments in every day that set the table for spiritual truth to be shared with a child. And perhaps the best time of all for sharing is bedtime. For many families, though, bedtime is the worst time of the day. It is often filled with tantrums and threats and tears. Though the parent may win this bedtime battle in the end, the parent's "victory" is, in truth, a loss. It results in a loss of peace. A loss of love. A loss of joy. It also results in a loss of memories that could have been created had the evening not ended in a battle of wills.

This little book may help change all that. It is designed to make bedtime a memorable time, a time both you and your child will look forward to.

In these pages you'll find a collection of stories, activities, games, and other fun things. Each ends with a short prayer you can pray aloud before tucking your child into bed. Feel free to use the prayer, or if you prefer, substitute one of your own. You may also ask your child to say a prayer, too.

Some of the evenings' activities require special props. These are listed at the top of the page so you can gather them ahead of time.

Some of these blessings are designed to show you care about the details of your child's life, reinforcing your concern through meaningful touch. Other blessings communicate a spoken message of love, and some convey your child's high value. Some activities reveal God's genuine commitment to your child. Still others express the special future that God has for your child.

Over the course of these 100 evenings, you will be giving your child a photo album of positive pictures. Of course, some of those pictures will fade from memory. But some will be remembered and treasured as long as your child lives.

What you are doing at bedtime will last a lifetime.

Maybe longer.

Lord willing, some day your child will grow up, get married, and have children of his or her own. Some of what you have imparted will be passed down to your grandchildren, and from them to their children, and from them—well, there's no telling how many generations will be affected by what you start tonight.

As you head out on this journey, may the Lord bless, keep and guide you and your family—now and for generations to come.

John Trent, Ph.D.
President, Encouraging Words
and Strongfamilies.com

The Blessings Box

Some of the blessings that follow require certain materials—mostly easy-to-find household items. These are listed at the start of each activity so you can gather them ahead of time. A complete list of all the supplies is provided here. If you wish, gather the supplies in a "blessings box" so you'll have them ready whenever you need them.

index cards
blunt scissors
pencils
paper
dollar or small gift
bar of Ivory soap
dull knife
cutting board
deck of cards
lemons
small drinking glasses
dull penny
lamp
small dish
toothpicks
two same-size cans of vegetables
matches
magnifying glass
shiny penny
notepad
old magazines
tape or glue

crayons
two large bowls
stationery
postage stamp
address book or phone book
colored pen or pencils
small pot
comic book
small potted plant
concordance
pictures of sunrises or sunsets
empty oatmeal box
flashlight
nail
coin
two large balloons
two rubber bands
washable markers
checkerboard and checkers
two bananas
two straight pins
watch or clock with second hand
cookbook with cookie section
large piece of poster board
thumb tacks
white butcher paper
mailing tube (for butcher paper)
child's story book
dictionary

LET'S PLAY A GAME
Treasure Hunt

[You will need a treasure, a treasure map, and several clues.]

[Before your child goes to bed, hide a small treasure in his or her room. The treasure can be a dollar or a small gift. It could be a coupon that your child can redeem, one where you offer your time for something he or she wants to do, such as going out for a hot-fudge sundae or a movie. Or you doing your child's chores for a week.]

[Next, draw an "X-marks-the-spot" treasure map that points to hidden clues. Be as creative as possible. For example: "Hangings take place there every day, yet no one has ever died," could hint at a clue placed in the closet. "Once there, you will be only a few feet from the next clue," can point to a clue hidden in a shoe.]

Let's go on a treasure hunt—right here in your room! This treasure map gives you all the clues you need.

[Once your child has found the treasure, tuck him or her into bed. Then place your hand on your child's head as you pray.]

Dear God,
Thank You for _____ *[your child's name]*. What a treasure he/she is to me. *[List specific reasons why your child is a treasure.]*
     Amen.

LET'S SING A SONG
Rock My Soul

Let's sing a song tonight. It's one we can do hand signs with, so it ought to be fun. Here are the words. Listen as I sing them.

> Rock my soul in the bosom of Abraham,
> Rock my soul in the bosom of Abraham,
> Rock my soul in the bosom of Abraham,
> Oh, rock-a-my soul.
>
> So high, you can't get over it,
> So low, you can't get under it,
> So wide, you can't get 'round it,
> Oh, rock-a-my soul.

The hand motions are pretty easy if you think about the words.

- **Rock:** Put your arms together as if you're rocking a baby.
- **Soul:** Bring your hands together and, going from bottom to top, move them over your body in one sweeping motion.
- **Bosom:** Put your hands over your chest.
- **Abraham:** "Draw" a capital A in the air.
- **Oh:** Bring your hands together to form an O shape.
- **High:** Lift up one hand as high as you can.

- **Over:** Make a gesture with your hand and arm as if you are pulling yourself up.
- **Low:** Push one hand down as low as you can go.
- **Under:** Use your hand and arm again, and pretend you are trying to pull something up from the ground.
- **Wide:** Spread your arms as far apart as you can.
- **'Round:** Make a motion with one hand going around in a circle.

[Talk through the lyrics and slowly practice the hand motions. When your child is ready, both of you start singing.]

Dear God,
Thank You for the gift of singing. It's a gift You've given only to the birds and to people. We feel so privileged to have it. Thanks again from both of us, _____ *[your child's name and yours].*
Amen.

LET'S MAKE SOMETHING
Soap Cross

[You will need a Bible, a bar of Ivory soap, a knife that isn't too sharp, and a cutting board.]

Is there anything we can do that's so bad God won't forgive us?

[Read aloud Psalm 51:1-3.]

These are words that David wrote after he broke God's laws and even had a man killed. But God forgave David. In the same way, He will forgive you for the bad things you do. Just tell Him what you did and ask Him to make your heart clean again.

As a reminder of how God cleanses us, let's make a cross out of this bar of soap.

[Let your child do the carving. When the cross is finished, let your child hold it as you put your hand on his or her hand and pray. The next day your child can use the soap cross to take a bath.]

Dear God,
May this cross remind _____ *[your child's name]* that at times we all think things and say things and do things that are wrong. But also remind _____ *[your child's name]* that You are always there to cleanse us of those things. In Jesus' name,
        Amen.

LET'S TELL A STORY
Alphabet Tales

[You will need a sheet of paper and a pencil.]

Tonight we're going to make up a story based on the letters of the alphabet. We'll say the letters together, and I'll write them on this sheet.

[Do this now, then explain the process.]

You can begin the story with any letter of the alphabet you want, but after that, you must follow the order of the alphabet. If you begin with the letter S, you have to go to the next letter—which is what? *(T)*

Here's how the game works. Say I start with the letter O. I make up a sentence that begins with that letter. For example:

"Once upon a time in a faraway land by the sea, there was a castle where a king, his daughter, and their housekeeper lived.

"Princess Delia was the daughter's name, and she was always sneaking out of the castle at odd hours during the night.

"Quietly one night, she got out of her bed, climbed down the trellis that led up to her window, and tiptoed out of the castle grounds, then ran to the seashore where she met—"

You get the idea. Now let's begin.

[You can create variations of this game by talking only about your family, or setting the story in a specific place— such as the desert—or you can restrict the subject to some- thing like food, as in the following example.]

"Alphabet soup is something I enjoyed as a child."

"Beef is what I like, especially when the beef is made into hamburgers."

"Can you tell me what you like to put on your ham- burger?"

Dear God,
Thank You for the fun times _____ *[your child's name]* and I have together. There is no place I would rather be than here. And thank You that even such a dull thing as the alphabet can be fun if only we use a little imagination.

    Amen.

LET'S PLAY A GAME
Tongue Twisters

Tongue twisters are sentences that are so difficult to say, it sounds as if you are talking with a twisted tongue.

Let's take turns doing a few. The first one is probably the most well-known of all tongue twisters:

> Peter Piper picked a peck of pickled peppers.
> A peck of pickled peppers, Peter Piper picked.
> If Peter Piper picked a peck of pickled peppers,
> Where is the peck of pickled peppers Peter Piper
>   picked?

For this second one, say it once, then try to say it five times as fast as you can.

> Fresh fish feel funny in your tummy.

The next tongue twister is:

> Rubber baby buggy bumpers.

Here's another one. Say it five times as fast as you can:

> Crow bait.

If your tongue isn't too tired, try this one five times as fast as you can:

> We reweave rips.

Okay, let's give our tongues a rest now.

Dear God,
Thank You that such small things as words can be so
much fun. May we always use our words wisely. In Jesus'
name we pray.
      Amen.

LET'S TALK ABOUT FEELINGS
Fear

[You will need a Bible.]

How we feel is important to God, especially when we feel afraid.

Can you think of some things that scare you? Of all these things, which do you most fear? Why?

[This conversation may provide an important opportunity to dispel your child's fears.]

The Bible says a lot about fear.

[Look up Psalm 23. Read verses 1-3 and point out the ways a shepherd cares for his sheep. Now read verse 4.]

David, who wrote this psalm, says we don't need to fear evil. Why?

[Explain why the shepherd's rod and staff should comfort us: The rod is like a club the shepherd uses to clobber predators like wolves. The staff is a hook-shaped walking stick the shepherd uses to pull a lamb out of a hole or scoop him out of the water.]

Let's pray.

Dear Lord,
Thank You that You are not just a shepherd, You are my
shepherd and _____'s *[your child's name]*
shepherd, too. Thank You for taking such good care of
us. When it gets dark, and we have to walk through difficult valleys, help us to see that we have nothing to be
afraid of—because You are walking right beside us.
        Amen.

LET'S PLAY A GAME
Story Cards

[You will need a deck of playing cards, or, if you prefer, "Old Maid" or "Go Fish" cards.]

Using this deck of cards we are going to make up a story. It could be a funny story or a sad story or a story filled with daring adventures and narrow escapes.

One of us will start the story by holding the deck of cards and picking a card from the top.

I might begin by drawing a king. I could start the story by saying: "Once upon a time there was a king who was so sad that he offered half his kingdom to anyone who could make him laugh. News of the offer went throughout the kingdom. So many people wanted a chance to win that the king had to schedule appointments for them all."

Now, when I want to pass the story to you, I give you the deck of cards, you pick one off the top, and with that card you continue the story. Say, for example, you choose a four of spades. You can use either the four or the spade or both. So, you might continue the story like this: "The very first appointment the king had was with four men, each carrying a shovel—"

Try to imagine something the four men could do with the four shovels that would cause the king to laugh. Or, you could just introduce the four men and pass the deck of cards back to me, and I would have to continue the story.

[Tell the story together until you reach a satisfying ending.]

Dear Lord,
Thank You for stories and the fun they give us. We thank You especially for the really great, true stories in the Bible, which are full of danger and adventure and heroic deeds. Help us to be heroes in the stories that we are telling others with our lives.
    Amen.

LET'S PLAY A GAME
Tic-Tac-Toe

[You will need paper and something to write with.]

This is an old game called Tic-Tac-Toe, and you play it with Xs and Os. You get to pick which letter you want. You win by putting three of your letters in a row. We take turns, but the one who has the Os goes first. Any questions? Okay, let's play.

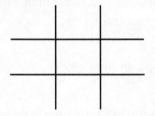

[To make the game a little more difficult, expand the size of the diagram. It still takes only three of your letters in a row to win.]

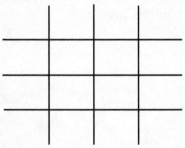

[Play as long as you want. Have fun and laugh together. Explain that the important thing about this bedtime activity isn't winning the game; it's spending time together.]

We had fun just being together tonight. Let's thank God for being here with us. We can also talk to Him about anything that's on your mind, whether it's a worry, a special need, or something else. What shall we pray about for you?

Dear God,
Thank You for _____ *[your child's name]*. Tonight I bring You what is on his/her heart. Especially I pray _____ *[finish by praying for what your child has shared with you]*.

Amen.

LET'S DO AN EXPERIMENT
Penny Bath

[You will need a lemon, a knife, a cutting board, a small glass of water, and a dull penny.]

[Cut the lemon in half.]

Let's squeeze this lemon's juice into the glass of water. I'll squeeze one half, you squeeze the other. Now you put this tarnished penny into the glass, and we'll see what happens.

[In about five minutes the coin will become like new.]

[While you're waiting, you can talk about the following.]

A lemon is a wonderful fruit. Can you think of some things we make from lemons?

[Lemonade; lemons add a crisp taste to iced tea; oil from the lemon rind is used in furniture polish, perfumes, and as a flavoring; a century ago lemons were used to fight the disease scurvy; lemon juice will remove mildew stains, rust stains, and even ink stains.]

You know, when man and woman were originally created, the Bible says they were created in "the image of God" (Genesis 1:27). They were like brand-new, shiny pennies. Then the man and the woman disobeyed God, and what do you think happened to them? They were tarnished by sin and lost their shine.

Then Jesus came. One of the reasons He came was to restore our "shine." And when we place our faith in Him, just as we place the penny in the juice, He sets about making us new.

[Fish out the penny and hold it in your hand.]

Like this.

Pretty neat, huh?

Dear God,
Thank You for sending Jesus to restore the shine that Adam and Eve had in the Garden of Eden before they sinned. Thank You that no matter how we have tarnished our lives, You are able to make each of us new again, clean again, shiny
again.
     Amen.

LET'S PLAY A GAME
I Spy

The name of tonight's game is I Spy. Here's how it's played. One of us goes first, then looks around the room and spies an object. Let's say you take the first turn. You begin the game by stating, "I spy something beginning with the letter S."

Then I ask a question: "Is it a shoe?"

If it's not a shoe, you answer, "No."

Then I continue the questioning: "Is it a sheet?"

And so on. You can start the clues a number of different ways. "I spy something that is red," or "I spy something that is small," or "I spy something that is plastic."

When I guess what you have spied, then it's my turn. Ready to play? Okay, look around the room until you spy something.

[When the game is over, hold your child's hands in yours while the two of you pray. Let your child go first, then you close with your prayer.]

Dear God,
Thank You for providing _____ 's *[your child's name]* room and for all the things in the room. You have been so kind and generous to us. Thank You so much.

Amen.

LET'S LEARN SOMETHING
What's in a Name

A long, long time ago nobody had a last name. But when people started living in towns, and as the towns grew, there were several Johns and several Toms and several Marys. This was confusing! So they came up with a way to make it very clear which person was being discussed.

If one of the Toms had a father named John, he was known as Tom, John's son, which in time became simply Tom Johnson.

If one of the Toms was a baker, he was known as Tom the Baker, which eventually became Tom Baker.

If Tom the baker married a woman named Mary, she would be called what? Mary the baker's wife. If they had a son named John, he would be called what? John Baker's son, which later became John Bakerson.

That's how last names came into being. People either used their father's first name or their profession or how they looked or where they lived.

If we still used that same approach to tell people apart, what would your name be?

The Bible says: "A good name is more desirable than great riches" (Proverbs 22:1). Since you and I have the same last name, it's up to both of us to keep it good. How can we do that?

[Talk about how our actions and attitudes show the world who we are inside.]

Dear Father in heaven,
Thank You for the good name that was given to me, and for the privilege of passing that good name to _____ *[your child's name]*. Help us to live in a way that is worthy of Your name, O Lord.
      Amen.

LET'S LEARN SOMETHING
The Power to Hurt

An ancient Greek philosopher once said this:

Although boys throw stones at frogs in sport,
the frogs do not die in sport but in earnest.
Bion [*280 B.C.*]

Tell me what you think this means.

[Allow your child to think this through. Don't be too quick to give the answer, but you can paint the picture so your child will see the meaning more clearly.]

This fable from an ancient Greek storyteller helps explain:

Some mischievous boys were playing on the edge of a pond, and, catching sight of some frogs swimming about in the shallow water, they began to amuse themselves by pelting them with stones, and they killed several of them. At last one of

the frogs put his head out of the water and said: "Oh, stop! Stop! I beg you. What is sport to you is death to us."
Aesop [*550 B.C.*]

Imagine those stones are being thrown not at frogs but at people. Now imagine that the stones aren't stones but words. How do we throw words at people in a way that is fun for us but hurtful to them? Have you been hurt by some words thrown at you? Tell me about it.

[Discuss this with your child.]

Now let's pray about the power of hurtful words.

Dear God,
Please help _____ *[your child's name]* to forgive those who have hurt him/her with their words. And please help us both never to use words in a way that will hurt another person. In Jesus' name we pray.
          Amen.

LET'S DO AN EXPERIMENT
Invisible Ink

[You will need a lamp, a lemon that is cut in half, two pieces of paper, a small dish, and two toothpicks.]

In tonight's experiment we are going to write with invisible ink. First we have to squeeze this lemon into the dish. Why don't you squeeze one half, and I'll squeeze the other? Now put your paper on a flat surface, then dip your toothpick into the lemon juice. Use the toothpick like you would a pencil and write a message or draw a picture with it. You'll have to dip your toothpick often because it doesn't hold much.

[You write something, too. When you both are finished, let the piece of paper dry for a minute.]

Now let's see if we can make the writing visible. Put yours up to the light bulb in the lamp.

[It should become visible in about a minute. Move the piece of paper around until all parts of the message or picture are revealed.]

Whoa! Amazing, huh? You can use this invisible ink to write secret messages or draw hidden pictures for your friends, if you like. That would be fun, wouldn't it?

Well, time for bed. Let's take a minute to pray. How about tonight we pray for one of your friends? Who would you pick? What, specifically, would you like to pray for?

You start; I'll finish.

Dear God,
Thank You for _____ *[the friend's name]*. We ask You to especially watch over this friend and please _____ *[offer your child's prayer request for this friend]*. We're glad You brought this friend to mind, just as the light brought our invisible ink into view.
        Amen.

LET'S SOLVE A PROBLEM
The Envelope Puzzle

[You will need a few pieces of paper and a pencil.]

[Before you go in to tuck your child into bed, draw this envelope on a piece of paper.]

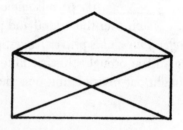

The problem you need to solve is to draw this envelope. That's not too hard, is it? Oh, I forgot. You can't lift your pencil off the paper. You can do that, can't you? Oh, one thing more. You can't retrace any of your lines.

[The answer is on page 198.]

Dear God,
Thank You for the brains You have given us to figure out problems like this. Help us to use these simple exercises to prepare us for bigger problems we may one day face. Please help _____ *[your child's name]* to solve every-day, ordinary problems with creativity and enthusiasm.
    Amen.

LET'S SING A SONG
A New Tune

[You will need a Bible.]

Let's sing a song—what do you say? I'll read a passage from the Bible, and we'll see if we can make up a tune to go with it.

[Read Psalm 23:1-4. Repeat it several times so your child will be familiar with the words.]

Try making up a tune.

[Give your child a chance to sing. If your child has trouble, help out by coming up with a tune of your own. Experiment with different tunes you might borrow, such as "Away in a Manger" or "Silent Night" or "Joy to the World." You may have to make some adjustments in the text to fit the tune, such as changing "green pastures" to "pastures green" or by using a verse as a chorus that you repeat.]

[Have fun creating your song and singing it together.]

Dear Lord,
It feels wonderful to sing to You. You are so worthy of all our songs, all our praise, all our worship. We love You. And we thank You for loving us.

Amen.

LET'S BE THANKFUL
Our Wonderful Bodies

Tonight we're going to look at our bodies.

Let's look at our hands first. Imagine what you couldn't do if you didn't have a thumb.

[You couldn't turn a doorknob. You couldn't throw a football at all. Have your child pick up a book. Now have your child fold down his/her thumb and try to pick up the same book.]

Let's look at our joints now. Imagine what it would be like if you didn't have joints. Stand up and stiffen all your joints with the exception of your hips and shoulders. Try walking. Now try picking something up. What do our joints do?

[They give us freedom of movement, allowing us to use our muscles and bones.]

Now let's pay attention to our eye sockets. Feel the bones around your eye. Why do you think our eyes are sunken into the sockets?

[Talk about how your eyes are protected from injury, surrounded by the strong bone of the skull.]

In Psalm 139:14, David says: "I praise you because I am fearfully and wonderfully made."

Let's do the same thing as we talk to God in prayer.

Dear Lord,
Thank You that _____ *[your child's name]* is fearfully and wonderfully made. Everything has a purpose. Every part of us exists either to serve us or to protect us. Tonight we especially thank You for our thumbs and our joints and the sockets around our eyes.

      Amen.

LET'S DO AN EXPERIMENT
Balancing Act

[You will need a small unbreakable drinking glass, an 8½ x 11-inch sheet of paper, and two same-size cans of vegetables.]

[Place the cans about six inches apart.]

Your challenge is to balance this glass between these two cans, using only this piece of paper to do it. You have two minutes to figure out how.

Give up?

Here, let me show you how it can be done.

[Take the piece of paper and lay it on a flat surface with the 11-inch side going horizontally. Now make folds in the paper, about half an inch thick, the way you would make a fan, going back and forth with your folds.]

Watch carefully.

[Put the folded paper on top of the two cans.]

Here.

[Give the glass to your child.]

You balance it.

In life we're sometimes faced with challenges that seem impossible. Few really are. Almost always there is a way to meet those challenges. Often we can't see how at first, but after we think about it, pray about it, and ask others for their ideas, the solution becomes clear. And many times, it's a lot easier than we first thought.

Do you have any challenges in your life that seem impossible?

[If so, talk about them. If not, close in prayer.]

Dear God,
Thank You so much for Your strength in the middle of life's difficulties. We know that You can help us deal with trouble, if we just remember to depend on You. *[Pray for your child's unique challenges, those mentioned as well as those unspoken.]*
Amen.

LET'S LOOK IN THE BIBLE
Burning Words

[You will need a Bible and a box of matches.]

[Read James 3:5.]

Why do you think James compares the tongue to a small spark or fire?

[Let your child share his or her thoughts.]

[Now light a match.]

A match is a small fire. If I let it keep burning, it would hurt my fingers.

[Blow the match out.]

What are some ways we can use a match? Misuse a match?

Words are like matches: They can help or hurt. Can you think of some good ways I have used words? What are some ways I have misused them?

What are some good ways you have used words? What are some ways you have misused them?

[Read James 3:9-12.]

James says our words can be a blessing or a curse. What does nature teach us about our words?

Are there some things we can do to control our tongues better? James has some good advice on that.

[Read James 1:19.]

Why do you think the Bible tells us to be "slow to speak"?

[We should think about what we say before we say it.]

What are some things that make us want to be quick to speak?

[Anger or other strong feelings can make us blurt out our thoughts before we realize how they might injure other people.]

Tonight why don't you pray about your tongue, and I'll pray about mine.

Dear God,
Please help me not only with what I say but how I say it. Help my words to warm _____ *[your child's name]*. And forgive me for the times my words have burned him/her. I'll try real hard to do better. In Jesus' name I pray.
           Amen.

LET'S LEARN SOMETHING
How to Whistle

There are many different ways to whistle, but I think this one is the easiest to learn.

Take your hand and stretch it out.

[Pick out the index finger for your child.]

This finger is called the index finger. Take it and the one next to it, and make a V. Good. Now put them in your mouth against your tongue. Like this.

[Show your child how to do it.]

Now try to whistle by blowing air through your fingers. This is going to be really fun, but it will take some practice.

[Work with your child till some degree of proficiency has been achieved.]

That was fun, wasn't it? It's a helpful thing to know because sometime you might need to get the attention of somebody who is far away, and whistling is a good way to do it.

Now let's pray. Tonight let's pray for our pastor. It's a hard job to do all the things a pastor has to do. They get tired just like anybody else. And discouraged. Even grumpy sometimes, just like you and me. It's important work he does, and we should pray for him regularly.

Dear God,
Thank You for our pastor. Help him with the work You have called him to do. Refresh him when he's tired. Encourage him when he gets discouraged. And cheer him up if ever he gets grumpy. He loves You, Lord. Help him to love You even more.

Amen.

LET'S PLAY A GAME
X Marks the Spot

This game will send shivers down your spine. Lie on your stomach.

[Raise your child's shirt and with your finger trace a big X, a big zero, and a small dot. While you are doing this, say, "X marks the spot, with a zero and a dot." Now quickly reach up and gently squeeze the back of your child's neck.]

Did you get the chills?

[Here is a variation of the game. If your child knows how to spell, trace a word on his or her back, not horizontally, but one letter of the word over the other. When you're finished, have your child guess the word. If your child can't read, trace a simple picture, like a tree or a cross or a bird.]

[Here's another fun touching game. Have your child sit up in bed and turn away from you. Tell your child not to worry, but you are going to crack an egg on his or her head. First, rest your fist on top of your child's head, simulating an egg. Now take your fist and slap it against your cupped hand, simulating the break. Uncurl your fist slowly, spreading your fingers down his or her head. It will feel remarkably similar to a broken egg.]

Those were fun things to do, weren't they? And now it's time for bed. And what should we pray about tonight? Why don't you think of something?

[When your child picks something, you might want to ask a few brief questions, such as, "Why would you like to pray about that?" or "Have you been feeling lately that God has been reminding you about that?"]

Okay, let's pray. You go first, then I'll close.

Dear God,
Tonight we especially pray _____ *[use what your child has chosen to pray about, and be specific in how you elaborate on it]*. In Jesus' name we pray.
      Amen.

LET'S TALK ABOUT WHEN I WAS YOUR AGE
Sharing Together

[After your child has answered the first two questions which follow, he or she gets to ask you the same ones.]

What is your favorite song? Why?

When I was your age, my favorite song was:

_____.

The reason why was:

_____.

What do you want to be when you grow up? Why?

When I was your age, I wanted to become a:

_____.

The reason why was:

_____.

What do you like most about your *[mom or dad—depending on which one you are]*?

Why?

When I was your age, what I liked most about my *[mom or dad]* was _____.

The reason why was:

_____.

What do you like least about me? Why?

[You may want to talk about this one.]

When I was your age, what I liked least about my *[mom or dad]* was:

_____.

The reason why was:

_____.

Dear God,
Thank You for this time of getting to know each other a little better. Thank You that _____ *[your child's name]* likes _____ *[what your child likes most about you]*. Help me with _____ *[what your child likes least]*. I'll work on that.
  Amen.

LET'S PLANT A SEED
Controlling Our Words

[You will need a Bible, an index card, and something to write with.]

The Word of God is like a seed (see 1 Peter 1:23). When God's Word is planted in our heart, it takes root, grows, and produces fruit that we can share with others. The way we "plant" it is to memorize it.

Tonight's verse is found in Proverbs 15:1.

[Read this verse, then write it on an index card.]

Why does a gentle answer turn away wrath?

[You may need to explain that wrath means anger.]

Why does a harsh word stir up anger?

Now let's plant the seed, okay?

[Read the verse along with its reference, and have your child repeat it. When you're done, put the index card in a prominent place. Pin it to a bulletin board, place it on a small stand, or use it as a bookmarker.]

Do you know how to water the seed? By praying the verse back to God. I'll show you how.

Dear God,
When people get angry at me, help me not to get angry back. Instead, help me to be calm and to respond with a gentle answer. It's a hard thing to do sometimes, so I'll need lots of help. Thank You ahead of time.
      Amen.

LET'S PLAY A GAME
Guess What?

In this game one person gets to think of an object while the other person tries to guess it. The person who thinks of the object has to give clues that have two parts: One part hints at what the object is; the other part says what it is not.

Suppose, for example, I think of an oven. The clues should be phrased like this: "I get hot, but I don't get angry. What am I?"

The other person has five guesses, one after each clue. If the person doesn't get the right answer by the fifth question, he loses, and the person giving the clues gets to go again. If the person guessing gets the answer right, it's his turn to think of an object.

Here's how we could continue with the oven example:

"I turn things brown, but I am not paint. What am I?"

"Every kitchen has one, but I am not a sink. What am I?"

"I need degrees to do my work, but I haven't gone to college. What am I?"

You get the idea. Now let me think of something, and you try to guess.

[Have fun taking turns, playing together until you are ready to pray.]

Dear God,
Thank You that You have revealed Yourself to us in the Bible so that we don't have to guess who You are, what You do, or what You require of us. You have made all of that so very clear, and we praise You for doing so. Please watch over _____ *[your child's name]*, and may all his/her dreams be sweet ones.

Amen.

LET'S TAKE A CLOSE LOOK
The Penny

[You will need a magnifying glass and a recently minted penny.]

[Use the magnifying glass to help your child study the back of the coin. Read the words.]

Have you ever heard what "E Pluribus Unum" means? *[It's Latin for "Out of many, one," referring to one nation made up of many people.]*

Do you know what building that is? *[It's the Lincoln Memorial in Washington, D.C.]*

Look closely. What do you see in the center of the building? *[It's very faint because the statue is set back from the columns, but it's a statue of Abraham Lincoln.]*

Let's turn the penny over. Whose image is on it? *[Lincoln's.]*

What date was this penny made?

Where was this penny made? *[D under the date is Denver; S is San Francisco; if there is no mint mark, it was Philadelphia.]*

[Look at the bottom edge of the bust to see V. D. B. The initials stand for Victor D. Brenner, who designed the coin.]

[Focus on the word "Liberty."]

What does that mean? Why do you think the idea of freedom is on the coin?

[Let your child share his or her ideas. Explain that our country was started by people seeking freedom.]

[Finally, point out the words "In God We Trust."]

Why do you think we have those words on the coin?

[The motto first appeared on a two-cent piece in 1864 at the suggestion of the Secretary of the Treasury. In 1955, Congress required all U.S. money to carry the motto. You might want to talk about the difference between trusting in God and trusting in money.]

Dear God,
Thank You for the nation we live in, one nation made up of many people, all of whom value freedom. Thank You for the religious freedoms we have here. And we especially thank You for the coin's motto, "In God We Trust." May it be our motto, too. And may it appear so clearly in our lives that others wouldn't need a magnifying glass to see it. In You we trust, Lord.
        Amen.

LET'S MAKE UP A STORY
In the Picture

[You will need several magazines you no longer want to keep, a pair of scissors, tape or glue, and several sheets of paper.]

Tonight we're each going make up a story that we can tell by using pictures from magazines. We'll both cut out about 10 pictures and glue them onto these pieces of paper. Once we have them all cut out and pasted, we'll take turns telling our stories.

[You may want to tell your story first to give your child an idea how it's done. Let your imagination flow. Try to think up ways to connect the characters and activities shown in your pictures. Is there a goal to be reached? A problem to be solved? A journey to be completed? Or maybe your story is just about a silly series of events. Have fun!]

Dear Lord,
Thank You for stories and the fun we have in making
them up and telling them. Thank You, too, for the story
You are making out of each of our lives, a story that is
largely made up of pictures rather than words. Help the
pictures we leave behind us show kind and loving
actions—creating images that will inspire others who
see them. In Jesus' name we pray.
    Amen.

LET'S DRAW A PICTURE
A Wild Animal

[You will need a box of crayons and a few blank sheets of paper.]

Tonight we're going to draw a picture together—but not just any picture. We are going to create a brand-new animal with our imaginations. And we'll make it out of the parts of other animals. I'll start with an idea, then you draw it. Then you come up with an idea, and we'll alternate like that until the animal is finished.

Ready to start? I'm imagining an animal that has the head and neck of a giraffe.

[When your child is finished drawing that, it will be his or her turn to come up with the next idea, which may be the body of a zebra, the feet of a duck, the tail of a horse, etc.]

Now let's give the animal a name.

Well, that was fun, wasn't it? Imagine how much fun God had in designing animals when He created the world. It all came out of His imagination and not from the parts of other animals, because animals hadn't been created yet. Pretty amazing, isn't it?

Why don't we spend some time giving thanks for the imaginations He gave us? You start, then I'll close.

Dear God,
It is amazing how You came up with so many wild and wonderful ideas when You created the earth and everything that went with it. Thank You for giving us the gift of imagination so we can feel how fun and exciting it is to create things—whether we're making up stories or creating anything from artwork to airplanes. We can see why You rested on the seventh day of creation to relax and enjoy looking at everything You made.

Amen.

LET'S TALK ABOUT THE DAY
Bedtime Quiz

Tell me about your day.

[As you ask this, provide an affirming touch by lightly brushing your fingertips up and down your child's arm.]

What did you eat?

Where did you go?

Who did you talk to?

What was the best part of your day?

Did anything make you angry or sad?

What did you learn?

Now brush your fingers over my arm, and you can ask me the same questions.

Let's pray. You give thanks for my day, and I'll give thanks for yours.

[You go first as this might be something that is unfamiliar to your child.]

Dear God,
[Use your child's answers to form your prayer.]

Amen.

LET'S PLAY A GAME
Right on Target

[You will need two large bowls and a deck of cards.]

[Place the bowls across the room.]

One bowl is for you and one is for me. In this game we evenly divide the deck of cards, and we take turns trying to throw one card at a time into our own bowl. The one with the most cards in the bowl wins.

You throw the card a little like you throw a Frisbee.

[Demonstrate.]

The first time we'll go through the deck as a practice round. The second time will be for real.

[If your child enjoys this, play several times.]

Okay, let's pick up all the cards, put you in bed, and pray.

[Hold hands as you pray.]

You know, when we pray, it's not like that game we just played, where some cards missed their target. God hears every single one of our prayers; there are no misses! Isn't that great? Why don't you thank God for something about today, then I'll pray and do the same.

Dear God,
Thank You for today. Thank You for _____ *[choose something about the day for which you are thankful, and weave that into your prayer]*. In Jesus' name we pray.
    Amen.

LET'S WRITE A LETTER
With Love From...

[You will need some stationery, a stamp, an address book or phone book, a Bible, and something to write with.]

Who would you like to write a letter to?

Let's write a bunch of questions and see if we get a letter back with the answers.

[If your child is too young to write, you do the writing, but let your child come up with the words.]

Okay, now that we're finished, we need to address the letter and include a return address.

Have we forgotten anything?

[The stamp. Let your child apply it, and the next morning let your child put it in the mailbox.]

You know, the Bible has a lot of letters in it. Most of them are from Paul to particular people, such as Timothy. Paul wrote two letters to Timothy. One is titled, "The First Epistle of Paul to Timothy," which we call "First Timothy." What do you think the word "epistle" means? *[Letter.]*

The other letter is titled, "The Second Epistle of Paul to Timothy," which we call what? *[Second Timothy.]*

Other letters are addressed to particular churches, like the one in Rome. It is titled, "The Epistle of Paul to the Romans."

[Read aloud how Paul's second letter to Timothy begins and ends, showing your child the verses, which are 1:1-2 and 4:19-22.]

Dear God,
We thank You for the letters in the Bible and for all the questions they answer about our faith. We thank You, too, for this letter_____ *[your child's name]* is sending to _____ *[the name of the recipient]*. We hope it makes his/her day, and that it will let this person know that he/she was in our thoughts today. We hope we hear something back.
          Amen.

LET'S HEAR A STORY
The Lion and the Mouse

Tonight we're going to hear another story by Aesop, the ancient storyteller who told fables, those short stories that teach important lessons about life. This one is called, "The Lion and the Mouse."

A lion was asleep in his den when a little mouse ran over his head, then down his face. The lion woke up and lost his temper. He slapped his big paw at the mouse and trapped his tail.

The mouse was terrified. "Please don't kill me. If you let me go, someday I will repay the kindness."

The idea that a little pip-squeak like a mouse could ever help a lion so amused the lion that he started laughing. The laughter put him in a better frame of mind, and he let the mouse go.

Time passed. One day the lion got tangled in a net that hunters had set out to capture wild animals. He roared so loudly, it shook the leaves on the trees. The more the lion tried to free himself, the more entangled he became, until at last he got so entangled that he couldn't move.

Hearing the roar, and sensing the lion was in danger, the little mouse scurried to find him. When he did, he remembered his pledge to the lion, and he started gnawing away at the net. One by one, he chewed through the ropes until at last the lion was free.

"There," said the mouse. "You laughed when I promised to help you, but now see the truth. Even a mouse can help a lion."

What is the moral of the story?

[Allow your child to think this one out. Then reveal it.]

The moral of the story is:

No act of kindness, no matter how small, is ever wasted.

No matter how small you are, _____ *[your child's name]*, you can make a difference in somebody's life. Did you know that? And no act of kindness, no matter how small, is ever wasted (see Matthew 6:2-4; 25:31-46).

Dear God,
Thank You for _____ *[your child's name]* and for all the small but significant things he/she does. And thank You that none of those kind things he/she does will be wasted. Thank You that You see them all, and that one day You will reward them all.
     Amen.

LET'S PRAY FOR SOMEONE
A Friend with Special Needs

Tonight let's pray for someone you know who has special needs. Who would that be?

What special needs does _____ *[the person's name]* have?

How do those needs affect how _____ *[the person's name]* feels about *[himself/herself]*?

How would you feel if you had those needs? How would it affect you? How would it affect the way you respond to those around you?

In the Bible, James talks about people with special needs. He says: "If a brother or sister is without clothing and in need of daily food, and one of you says to them, 'Go in peace, be warmed and be filled,' and yet you do not give them what is necessary for their body, what use is that?" (James 2:15-16, NASB).

Can you think of something we could do that would help with _____'s *[the person's name]* needs?

[If so, make plans to do it.]

Let's pray. You pray first, then I'll pray.

Dear God,
Thank You that You care for those whose needs are desperate. You care for the widow and the orphan. You care for the hungry and the homeless. You care for the sick and for those who are sad. Tonight we would like to bring before You someone we care about who has special needs. We pray for _____ *[the person with special needs]*. Especially we pray _____ *[use specifics from your child's answers]*.

      Amen.

LET'S IMAGINE
Drawing Mind Pictures

Get under your covers and rest your head on your pillow.
I'll lie down next to you on top of the covers. Now close
your eyes, and I will close mine. We're going to spend
time imagining—drawing beautiful, fun, and interesting
pictures in our minds. The pictures can be still, like a
drawing, or filled with action.

What would you like to imagine?

[Allow your child to choose anything, then ask questions.]

Look closely at the picture in your mind. What do you
see? How do you feel about what you see? Why do you
think you feel that way?

What is your favorite part about what you see?

Why do you think you chose that to think about?

Okay. Now I'll imagine something, and you ask me any
questions you like.

[When your child is done, you both can open your eyes.]

Imagining is fun, isn't it? Why do you think God gave us
our imaginations?

[Let your child give his or her opinion.]

One of the reasons is that imagination is necessary for us to have faith. The Bible says that "faith is the assurance of things hoped for, the conviction of things not seen" (Hebrews 11:1, NASB). It goes on to say that it is "by faith we understand that the worlds were prepared by the word of God, so that what is seen was not made out of things which are visible" (verse 3).

When we look back to the past or forward to the future, we have to use our imaginations to see. The whole spiritual world, in fact, is filled with things we can't see. We can't see angels, for example, unless they reveal themselves to us. Just as we can't see the wind but only the effects of the wind, so we can't see the Holy Spirit, only the effects of the Holy Spirit as He works in us and around us.

[Remind your child that when you pray, you are talking to God, even though you can't see Him. He is always there, and always listening.]

Dear God,
It's frustrating sometimes that we can't see what You have done in the world, what You will someday do, or what You are doing now. Help us to imagine what You have told us in Your Word. And in our imaginings, help us to believe. In Jesus' name we pray.
        Amen.

LET'S PRETEND
Crazy Questions

This is a game with lots of questions, but no answers. You have to respond to a question with a question. If you answer a question, the game is over. To make a trial run, let's pretend that you live in this house, and I am a neighbor who comes to the door to borrow something.

I knock on the door, and you answer it. Before you get a chance to say anything, I ask you a question—something like this: "Do you have a cup of sugar I can borrow?"

If you answer the question by saying "yes" or "no," the game is over.

You have to answer the question with a question. So our conversation would go something like this:

"Do you have a cup of sugar I can borrow?"

"Why in the world would you want to borrow a cup of sugar?"

"Why is that important to you?"

"Why wouldn't it be?"

"Well, will you or won't you?"

"Will you tell me first why you want it?"

"Will you stop asking that?"

"Why, does it bother you?"

You get the basic concept. Any questions before we begin? Okay, let's pick a setting and the characters we want to play.

[Play until you decide it's time to stop, or you are both laughing so hard you can't go on.]

Okay, time for beddy-bye. Tonight, why don't you say the prayer all by yourself?

[Let your child pray.]

LET'S MAKE A WISH
Learning to Be Thankful

[You will need a Bible.]

If you had only one wish, and you knew the wish was going to be granted, what would it be?

If you had one wish for Mommy, what would it be?

If you had one wish for Daddy, what would it be?

If you had one wish for our family, what would it be?

What do you think God's wish is for us? Why don't we look in the Bible to see if we can find it?

[Read 1 Thessalonians 5:18.]

Let's pray and take those wishes to God.

[Place your hand on your child as the two of you pray.]

You pray first, then I'll go after you.

Dear God,
Thank You that we can come to You with anything.
Tonight we come to You with our wishes. For Mommy
we wish _____ *[use the child's wish]*. For Daddy
we wish _____ *[your child's wish]*. For our family
we wish _____ *[your child's wish]*. For _____
[your child's name] we wish _____ *[your child's
wish]*. And for both of us we wish what You wish for us:
that we give thanks in all things, which is not always
easy. So we'll need Your help. In Jesus' name we pray.
    Amen.

LET'S TALK ABOUT GOD
Three in One

[You will need a glass of water, a glass of ice, and a small pot of water that has been boiled and has steam coming from it.]

[Set the glasses and the pot on a night stand or other flat surface in your child's room.]

We know from reading the Bible that there is one God, but this God is made up of three persons: God the Father, God the Son, and God the Holy Spirit.

It's a mystery how there can be three persons but only one God, but this illustration may help you understand it.

How are the contents of these two glasses and one pot the same? *[They are all water.]*

How are the contents different? *[One is a solid, one is a liquid, and the other has steam, a gas.]*

They are all water, yet they are three different forms of the water: a solid, a liquid, and a gas.

God as three persons in one—Father, Son, Holy Spirit—can be difficult to understand, and no one understands it fully. But does this illustration help you picture God a little more clearly?

[Encourage your child if he or she is still confused. It may take time to grasp this concept, but as your child grows, the concept of three-in-one will become more understandable.]

Now let's pray.

Dear God,
You are so big and we are so small. Trying to look at You from the place of our smallness, we have a hard time seeing just how big You really are. We thank You for the illustrations in nature that teach us things about life, and especially for those that show us more about You. Thank You that tonight we have come to understand You a little better. Keep teaching us, Lord. We have so much to learn.
　　　　Amen.

LET'S LOOK AT NATURE
How Do Plants Eat?

[You will need a small potted plant.]

People get food into their bodies in one way. What is it? *[Through the mouth.]*

Plants, though, get their food in two ways. What do you think those are? *[From their leaves and from their roots.]*

When the sun shines on the leaves, it helps to make chlorophyll, the substance that makes the leaves green. The leaves take in something in the air called carbon dioxide. Oxygen is what we inhale. Carbon dioxide is what we exhale. It is just the opposite with plants. They breathe in carbon dioxide and breathe out oxygen. When the sunlight hits the plant's leaves, it activates the chlorophyll—the substance that gives leaves their green coloring—and turns the carbon dioxide and water in the leaves to carbohydrates, which is food for the plant.

The plant's roots, on the other hand, dig into the earth. There the roots draw water and minerals from the soil, sending them up the stem to nourish the plant.

Part of the plant lives in the air. Another part of it lives in the soil. This is similar to how we live. Your body is nourished by things from the earth. Your soul is nourished by things from heaven.

If you don't eat, what happens to your body? *[It starves.]*

If you're not being nourished by spiritual things, what happens to your soul? *[It starves, too.]*

You know what to do to feed your body, but what do you do to feed your soul? *[Pray, read the Bible, memorize Bible verses, attend church or Sunday school, help the poor, learn about God from parents, or any other ideas you have.]*

Dear God,
Thank You for giving _____ *[your child's name]* a body and for giving him/her a soul. Help us to take good care of them both. Thank You for our bedtime talks together as we learn about You, feeding our souls so we can grow to be the people You want us to be.
     Amen.

LET'S TALK ABOUT THE FUTURE
The King Is Coming

[You will need a deck of cards.]

[Take out one of the kings from the deck, then put the deck in front of your child.]

This game is called The King Is Coming.

[Show your child the king you removed.]

Here is the king so you will know what to look for.

[Now put the king back in the deck, and shuffle the cards.]

What you need to do is predict when the king is coming. You may want to guess the third card, or you may want to guess the middle of the deck, or maybe the end.

Okay, tell me when you think the king is coming.

[Go through the deck, card by card, until you find the king. When you do, you stop and take a minute to discuss the Second Coming of Christ.]

The Bible says that Jesus, the King of Kings, is going to come back to earth someday. It's called the Second Coming of Christ. The Bible also says that no one knows the date or the time of day He is coming, not even the angels.

What do you think it will be like, seeing Jesus for the first time?

How happy do you think He will be to see us?

How happy will you be to see Him?

I'm going to leave this card that has the king on it in your bedroom so that you will be reminded of His coming. From time to time you can pray that Jesus comes soon and makes all things beautiful again.

Dear Jesus,
Thank You for coming to the earth some 2,000 years ago. You came like a common person. But when You come again, You will come like a king. What a wonderful kingdom You will rule over one day. We feel so privileged that You have chosen us to be a part of it all. We so look forward to seeing You. Come soon. From
_____ [your child's name]
and _____ [your name].
       Amen.

LET'S READ TOGETHER
Comic Book Cuddle

[You will need to buy a comic book, one that is age-appropriate for your child.]

I bought this for you.

[Give the comic book to your child.]

Would you like me to read the words while you follow along with the pictures?

[If your child is now a reader, you may want to divide up the story's characters and take turns reading their dialogue.]

[Cuddle next to your child and read the comic book, stopping here and there if your child wants to point out something or ask a question.]

Dear God,
Thank You for the fun we had tonight in reading this comic book together. The best part of that for me was not the comic book itself, but cuddling next to
_____ *[your child's name]* and just being together.
Thank You that we can share these special times at bedtime.

      Amen.

LET'S LOOK IN THE BIBLE
Finding Answers

[You will need a Bible and a concordance.]

Let's look up some Bible verses that help answer questions you are curious about or give God's guidance on things you might be concerned about.

[Let your child ask one question or tell one concern at a time. If your child has trouble getting started, you might ask questions to draw out how he/she has been feeling about recent events in your family or challenges and changes coming up in the near future.]

[For each, look in the concordance to find some appropriate Scripture verses. Then read the verses from the Bible and discuss them. Take as many questions as you feel you have time for, then tuck your child into bed.]

Dear God,
Thank You that You haven't left us here to figure everything out on our own. Thank You for giving us Your Word, which speaks to us about so many of our problems, questions, and the things that concern us. We really appreciate it.
     Amen.

LET'S PRETEND
If Animals Could Talk

[You will need a Bible.]

Do you know that in the Bible there is a story about a talking animal? It's found in Numbers 22:21-34.

[Read the story about Balaam's donkey.]

Suppose all animals could talk. What do you think they would say?

Let's pretend they do speak, and let's ask them some questions.

[You ask the question and let your child answer it. Then alternate.]

Deer, what is it you would like to say to humans?

Dog, what is it you would like to say?

Cat, how about you?

Now let's ask more specific questions. I would like to ask the giraffe something.

Giraffe, I bet when you get a sore throat, it's a humdinger. I can see how your long neck is helpful in eating the leaves of tall trees, but is it a problem when you get a drink? How do you do it?

Which animal would you like to talk to? What question would you want to ask?

[You can do this as long as you like, until you run out of questions or run out of time. If you want to discuss a few things the Bible has to say about how we should treat animals, see Proverb 12:10, Deuteronomy 25:4, Exodus 20:8-10, Leviticus 25:1-7.]

Dear God,
Thank You for creating the animals. Help us to treat them kindly and gently. And help us to understand them, what they need, what they are afraid of, and what they would want to say to us if only they could talk. In Jesus' name we pray.

   Amen.

LET'S HAVE A RIDDLE
Quick Riddles

Tonight we're going to have some fun with riddles. Let's try to solve these together, okay?

[If you can't figure them out, the answers are on page 198.]

1. What did one wall say to the other?

2. What did the carpet say to the floor?

3. What has eyes but cannot see?

4. What has ears but cannot hear?

5. What has a tongue but cannot speak?

6. What has feet but cannot walk?

7. What has roots but no leaves?

8. What belongs to you but is used mostly by your family and friends?

9. Which is faster, heat or cold?

10. Under what circumstances is it okay to lie?

11. When can a broken watch tell the right time?

12. What can you brush but you cannot comb?

13. What can you pick but you cannot choose?

14. What can you tell without using words?

15. What asks no questions but you always have to answer?

Riddles are fun because they challenge us to figure out the right answers. Sometimes we laugh because the answers seem so simple. Aren't you glad we had the answers to these riddles in the back of the book, so we weren't left wondering?

Now, guess who knows every answer to every question there is. Of course, it's God! Let's talk to Him now.

Dear God,
Thank You for this time with _____ [your child's name] to think and to realize that often the answers to life's riddles lie right in front of us. Help us to see Your answers clearly.
        Amen.

LET'S WRITE A LETTER
With Thanks

[You will need some stationery or thank-you notes, something for the two of you to write with, and a flat surface to write on.]

Tonight let's write a letter or two. Try to think of a person who has had a big influence in your life, either for teaching you something or setting a good example. Or think of someone who has been especially kind to you. I'll do it, too.

Let's start thinking and we'll see which person God brings to mind.

[Once you and your child come up with a name, talk about why that person has been special. Then write a letter thanking that person for specific ways he or she has helped your child. If your child can't write, you could take dictation and write the letter yourself, using your child's words. Write as many of these letters as you want or as time allows.]

Aren't you glad about the people God has placed in your life? Let's thank Him now for all they have done for us.

Dear God,
Thank You for the special people in my life and the life
of _____ *[your child's name]*. Thank You for all
they've taught us, all they've shown us about
patience and love and kindness, and what
good examples they've been. Help us
also to be special people in the
lives of others.

    Amen.

LET'S PLAY A THINKING GAME
Clues

This is a game called Clues. From the clues I give, you have to guess what I am. I may be an animal, a vegetable, or even something related to weather—say, a tornado. I may be something you would find at a store, in your room, or at the playground.

When it's your turn, you can be anything you want to be. Just don't tell me! All you can do is give me clues, up to 20 of them. If I haven't guessed after 20, I'm done, and you can reveal what you were. If I can't guess what you are, you get to do it again. But if I discover who you are, it's my turn to give clues.

I'll give you an example. Suppose I decide to be "an airplane." Here are some clues I might give you: I am made of metal. I used to be made of wood. I've been all over the world. People use me sometimes when they go on vacations. And so on.

[You start off the game, choosing to be "ice." Below are the clues.]
1. I am solid.
2. I can be crushed.
3. I can be shaved.
4. I can be dry.
5. I help preserve things.
6. In the early part of the 1900s, I was delivered to houses.

7. I can be sharp enough to cut you.
8. Sometimes you can see through me.
9. I can be found at parties.
10. I can be found in nature.
11. I can cover things.
12. I can be found in your home.
13. I usually come in winter.
14. I am a solid.
15. I am cold.
16. I sometimes come in storms.
17. People sometimes make sculptures out of me.
18. You don't want to drive on me.
19. I'm sometimes found in trays.
20. Skaters love me, skiers hate me.

[Take turns playing as many times as you like.]

Dear Jesus,
You have revealed Yourself to us in many different ways:
through the Bible; through other people; through the
church. When I think of "I am," I think of You and all the
clues You have given us, clues which show Your true self.
You told us, "I am the good shepherd. I am the resurrec-
tion and the life. I am the way, the truth, and the life. I am
the light of the world." Sorry it has taken the world so
long to figure out who You really are. Please keep on
revealing Yourself to us, and we'll keep on trying to understand who You are and how we can be more like You.

     Amen.

LET'S PLAY A GAME
Funny Bunny

Tonight's game is Funny Bunny. Funny Bunnies are word-pairs that rhyme. Like "funny bunny" or "kitten's mittens."

Here's how you play. One person thinks of a Funny Bunny, and then gives a clue so the other person can guess what it is. For example, I might be thinking of a "hoarse horse." My clue would be: "animal with a sore throat." Or, I tell you I'm thinking of an "animal's chuckle." The right answer would be a "calf's laugh."

Okay, I'll start.

[Here are a few to get you going:

tin bin,

rat hat,

boy's toys,

dollar collar,

mouse house,

bear chair.]

Wasn't that fun? Let's see if we can think of Funny Bunny nicknames for each of us, before we spend time talking to God.

[Use your first names, family names—Dad, Mom, Son, Daughter—or other words that describe you to create your rhyming nicknames.]

Dear God,
Thank You for _____ *[your child's name]* and our family and the care You provide for each one of us. Watch over us as we sleep and refresh us so tomorrow we can be alert to all the blessings You have in store for us.

Amen.

LET'S PLAY A GAME
Squiggles

[You will need some crayons and several pieces of paper.]

This game is called Squiggles. One of us draws a squiggle or some kind of line-shape on a piece of paper. It is the other person's job to make a picture out of it.

For example, one person might draw a squiggle like this:

Then the other player turns the squiggle into a picture, like this:

[Go back and forth as many times as you like until it's time to pray and say goodnight.]

Dear God,
Thank You for the beautiful work You do in this world. We know You can make sense out of things that are confusing and difficult for us to understand. Thank You for the way You help people through natural disasters like earthquakes and floods, in time making everything beautiful again. For You, I'm sure, it's as easy as this game of Squiggles. Still, we thank You for it. In Jesus' name we pray.

Amen.

LET'S SING
Row Your Boat

[You will need a notepad and something to write with.]

Just for fun, let's sing a song. How about this one?

> Row, row, row your boat,
> Gently down the stream.
> Merrily, merrily, merrily, merrily,
> Life is but a dream.

To make it a little more interesting, let's keep that tune but change the words. Like this:

> Fly, fly, fly away,
> High up in the sky.
> Hungrily, hungrily, hungrily, hungrily,
> I think it's time for pie.

Now let's make up our own words.

[Jot down your ideas. You will need words that can be repeated, words that rhyme, and words that have the same number of syllables as each line of the song above. This can be a fun exercise that will build your child's creativity, word skills, and musical skills. When you're finished, try singing

your new song together. Another time you may want to come up with more new words to create songs that fit this tune.]

You are such a creative person! Don't you enjoy creating something new? I do, too! Now let's talk to God.

Dear God,
It's fun to create a new song out of our own words and then sing it. I hope we can do that with the thoughts we have in our heart for You. Help us turn those thoughts into words, and those words into a song of life that honors You. May we sing it with great love and much joy.
Amen.

LET'S WRITE SOMETHING
Rhyme Time

[You will need some index cards and something to write with.]

[Beforehand, write a number of words that rhyme on some index cards. Only write one word on each card. Do about four pairs of words.]

I'm going to put these rhyming words on the floor, and the first thing you have to do is pair up the ones that rhyme. Ready, go.

[If your child can't read, you read the words.]

Now let's see if you can make a poem out of these words.

[If your child doesn't know what a poem is, read one, like the song "Row, row, row your boat," or "Hickory, dickory, dock." Give your help when it is needed.]

Why are rhymes so much fun?

[They make us smile; they please our ears; they help us remember things, too.]

Have you ever stopped to realize that God created us with a wonderful ability to appreciate words and ideas? The world which He made is filled with rhythms and patterns that repeat like rhyming words in a poem or song. Where do we see and hear these rhythms in our world?

[Let your child think and answer. Possibilities include: the changing seasons; the waves on the shore; the phases of the moon; dawn and dusk; and so on.]

Shall we thank God for this amazing world He has given us?

Thank You, Lord.
Help us to see all the poetry that You have created in our world: The pleasing rhythms of waves lapping the shore. Sunrise, sunset. The rhythms of the seasons. Sundays and holidays. Help us to be better listeners and learners so we won't miss anything You have provided for us.
      Amen.

LET'S LOOK AT NATURE
Our Colorful Sun

[If you have pictures of sunrises or sunsets that show the sun in different colors, that would be helpful, but it isn't necessary.]

Do you ever wonder why the sun changes colors during the course of the day? It may be orange-colored in the morning or maybe pinkish. It's yellow as it rises and descends, whitish at noon, and often golden or slightly red at sunset.

Can you guess why?

[Let your child answer.]

In fact, the sun doesn't change colors at all. It remains the same. What changes is how we see the light. In the early morning and the late afternoon, the light of the sun is filtered through the earth's atmosphere. The atmosphere can be full of things, such as dust and tiny particles. When the sun shines through them, the light is reflected by these particles, and, depending on the type of particles, we may see any number of colors. As the sun rises higher, we don't see its reflection off these particles, so it appears brighter and more white.

That is the same reason stars appear to sparkle. Particles in the atmosphere are constantly moving, making the twinkling effect. The fewer particles there are in our atmosphere, the less stars seem to sparkle. The more particles, the more the stars twinkle.

Did you know that in the Bible the sun is used as an example of God's faithful love (see Psalm 136:1-9)? Without the sun, the earth would immediately turn so cold that everything would die. But as a sign of His faithful love for us and His creation, it comes up every day, like clockwork.

Let's thank God for the way He faithfully loves us.

Dear God,
We thank You for the sun and the moon and the stars. How beautiful they are to look at. But more importantly, they remind us of the faithfulness of Your love—not just to us but to every living thing You've created. Help us to love You back the same way.
        Amen.

LET'S PLAY A GAME
Rock, Scissors, Paper

This is a very old game, but a good one. It's called Rock, Scissors, Paper. Here's how you play. Put one of your hands behind your back, and outstretch the other before you with your flattened palm turned upward.

With the hand behind your back, you can do one of three things: Make a rock by balling your hand into a fist; make a piece of paper by stretching your hand out flat; or make a scissors by forming your index finger and the one next to it in a V sign.

Once you've made one of these with your hand and I've done the same, we count together: "One, two, three." When we get to three, quickly pull your hand from behind your back and slap it onto the outstretched hand in front, revealing that you have either a rock or paper or scissors. We do this at the exact same time.

Here's how you win. Remember these guidelines: Rock dulls scissors. Scissors cut paper. Paper wraps rock. So if you have scissors and I have paper, you win. But if you have scissors and I have a rock, I win.

Do you understand? Any questions? Okay, let's start: "One, two…"

[Play this game as many times as you want. And remember, the faster you slap your hand down, the more fun it becomes.]

Dear God,
Thank You for games and the fun we have playing them. It's especially fun to play them with someone we love. Please watch over _____ *[your child's name]* and help him/her have a good night's sleep. We love You. Goodnight from _____ *[your child's name and your name]*.

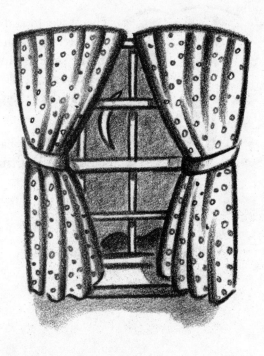

LET'S PLAY A GAME
Memory Challenge

This is a memory game. I'll start by saying something like: "I am going to the store to buy some bread."

Then you add something to the list, but first you have to repeat what I've said, so you would say something like this: "I am going to the store to buy some bread and a head of lettuce."

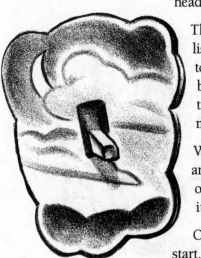

Then I would add to the list, saying, "I am going to the store to buy some bread and a head of lettuce and a gallon of milk."

We keep going back and forth like that until one of us forgets an item on the list.

Okay, let's play. You start.

[If your child is enjoying the game, play as many rounds as you have time available.]

Now we'll make another kind of list: all the things we want to thank God for.

Let's pray by taking turns, going back and forth as we mention things in our lives that make us thankful. This time, though, we don't need to repeat what the other person has said.

[When you run out of ideas for your list, finish the prayer by saying "Amen."]

LET'S LOOK AT NATURE
Butterfly Lessons

Nature is the work of God, and as with any other artist, you can see something of God in the art He has produced.

God has revealed Himself in His creation, and He has created things in the animal and plant world which teach us important lessons.

• Solomon learned something from the ant (Proverbs 6:6-8).

• David discovered something from trees (Psalm 1:1-3).

• Jesus taught using illustrations from nature. "Do not be anxious for your life, as to what you shall eat....Look at the birds of the air, that they do not sow, neither do they reap, nor gather into barns; and yet your heavenly Father feeds them. Are you not worth much more than they?" (Matthew 6:25-27, NASB).

• The apostle Paul uncovered some lessons from nature, too (see 1 Corinthians 15:35-44).

Let's take a look at the butterfly and find out what it can teach us. The butterfly is so beautiful with its delicate wings and its bright colors. And it flies from flower to flower so effortlessly. But do you know how a butterfly starts out? As a caterpillar, which is kind of like a big, fat worm. It is not very pretty. It can't fly. It just pokes along.

Then it makes a cocoon, and in it the caterpillar turns to liquid before the cells start building a new creature. After the new creature is formed, it breaks out of the cocoon, and—voila!—it's a butterfly.

What lesson do you think God is trying to teach us through the butterfly?

[Here are a few options you can talk about. In John 3 we learn we must be born again to enter God's kingdom. Second Corinthians 5:17 tells us we are new creatures in Christ. First Corinthians 15:50-53 describes the new bodies we will someday receive.]

Dear God,
Thank You that everywhere we look, there are signs of You, especially in nature. Your whole creation speaks of You, and as it does, it teaches us something, too. Thank You for that. Give us eyes to see and hearts to understand that You are using all the wonderful things in nature to teach us about Yourself.

Amen.

LET'S PLAY A GAME
Concentration

[You will need a deck of cards. Playing cards would work, or you could use cards for "Old Maid," "Crazy Eights," "Go Fish," or any others with duplicate pictures or numbers.]

Tonight we'll play a game called Concentration.

[Shuffle the cards, and put them face down on the bed, arranged in a square or a rectangle.]

The game begins when the first player turns over any two cards to see if they match. If they do, the player gets to keep the cards and gets another turn. If they don't match, the player turns the cards back over and the turn passes to the other player.

We keep going until all the cards are matched. The player with the most cards wins.

[*For younger children, you should lay out a smaller square, using fewer cards. Older children can handle a bigger playing "board."*]

[*Explain that a game like Concentration demonstrates how important it is to pay attention. Your child wouldn't have remembered any of the matches without focusing and thinking hard—concentrating!*]

It's good to think hard and exercise our minds, isn't it? Now let's concentrate on God as we talk to Him.

Dear God,
Thank You for our minds that allow us to think and concentrate. Help us to have that same concentration each day, but remind us to concentrate on things that are important, like kindness and gentleness and love. Give both of us a good night's sleep tonight, we pray, so that
_____ [*your child's name*] and I will wake up refreshed and better able to concentrate on the things that matter. In Jesus' name we pray.
   Amen.

LET'S MAKE SOMETHING
A Ceiling of Stars

[You will need an empty oatmeal box, a flashlight, a pair of scissors, and a nail. If you have a star chart or some reference book that shows the constellations, you'll find it helpful.]

Tonight we're going to take off the ceiling of your room and look at the stars. That would be fun, wouldn't it?

Here's what we're really going to do. Take this nail and punch several small holes in the oatmeal box top. These are going to be our stars. You can arrange them any way you want. How about putting them in clusters or in constellations? That's how stars are arranged in the sky.

[If you have a book that shows constellations, show it to your child and explain some of them. Ask your child to pick one or two for the oatmeal lid.]

After you punch out stars, I'll take this pair of scissors and cut a hole in the bottom of the oatmeal box just large enough for the flashlight to fit through.

[Do so. When you're both finished, put the lid back on the box. Push the flashlight through the bottom of the box, pointing up.]

You hold the flashlight now, ready to shine the light through the stars on the lid and onto the ceiling. But don't turn it on until I tell you.

[Go to the door, shut it, then turn off the light.]

You can turn it on now.

[Talk with your child about the stars as you enjoy the star-lit ceiling.]

It may not be quite as big and beautiful as the real starry sky, but our ceiling tonight reminds us of God's amazing power. How wonderful that He scattered the stars across the night sky. And yet, for all His mighty power, God loves little people like us; He loves you and He loves me. Let's thank Him now.

Dear God,
Your Word says that the heavens are declaring the glory of God and that night after night they display knowledge (Psalm 19:1-2). How quietly the stars speak of Your glory, but how clearly they communicate. Thank You for them, for all they have to say to us, and for how beautifully they say it.

Amen.

LET'S THINK ABOUT SOMETHING
Our Generous God

[You will need a glass of milk, which you can give your child with a few cookies as a bedtime snack, if you want.]

Let's take a good look at this glass of milk.

Where did it come from? *[Mom or Dad bought it.]*

Where did Mom or Dad get it? *[From the store.]*

Where did the store get it? *[From a person in a truck that delivered it.]*

Where did the delivery person get it? *[From a warehouse.]*

Where did the warehouse get it? *[From another person who delivered it there.]*

Where did that delivery person get it? *[From a dairy farm.]*

Where did the dairy farm get it? *[From a cow.]*

Where did the cow get it? *[From the grass and the water it eats.]*

Where did the grass and the water come from? *[From the earth.]*

Where did the earth get the grass and the water? *[From God.]*

If we take anything and trace it far back enough, all good things lead to God (see James 1:17).

Now you take a book from your shelf and trace it back to its beginning. Start with the person who gave it to you.

Dear God,
Thank You that every good gift comes from Your hand. Help us see that it doesn't matter how many other hands it comes through to get to us; if we follow the hands back far enough, the gift starts out in Your hands. Thank You for taking such good care of us. Help us to look carefully so we can see Your hand more often and thank You for all the good things that wind up in our hands.
        Amen.

LET'S PLAY A GAME
Balloon Volleyball

[You will need a coin and a large balloon or two, in case one pops.]

There are all kinds of things you can do with balloons. Tonight let's use one as a ball. We're going to play Balloon Volleyball.

First we have to blow up the balloon. Here, you do it, okay?

[Let your child at least try. If it's too hard, you can finish blowing it up. One thing you can do to make blowing up the balloon easier is to stretch the balloon a few times to limber it up. Also explain to your child how to tie the knot on the end.]

We'll need a net. Let's see, what can we use for a net? How about this chair?

[Use whatever is handy to serve as a net. But don't make any out-of-bounds markers. It will be hard enough to hit the balloon over the chair.]

The rules are: One of us serves while the other one receives the serve. You get to hit the balloon only one time to get it over the net. If you are the one serving and the balloon you hit doesn't make it over the net, the serve goes over to me. If I make it over the net and you miss it, then I get a point. Only the server gets points. Any questions?

Let's flip a coin to see who serves first. Call it in the air, heads or tails.

Let's play.

[Play short games of, say, five points each. Shorter games tend to be more fun.]

Okay, bedtime. Why don't you pray tonight? What would you like to pray about?

[You may want to ask questions about your child's prayer requests or to comment briefly on them.]

[Let your child pray aloud.]

LET'S READ A STORY
David and Goliath

[You will need a Bible—a kid-friendly translation.]

Tonight we're going to read an adventure story—one about a young boy. His name is David. He grew up to be Israel's greatest king. But he started out as an ordinary boy, except for one thing: He really and truly and deeply loved God.

It's an exciting story, and it's found in the book of the Bible called First Samuel.

[Read the story in 1 Samuel 17:1-51.]

Wow! That David was sure a brave boy, wasn't he? What part of the story did you like best?

[Let your child respond.]

I would like to have David's courage, wouldn't you? How do you think he became such a courageous person?

[Point out that David's great faith helped him take on the nearly impossible task of beating a giant. David knew God would help him.]

In Romans 8:31 we read, "If God is for us, who can be against us?" The story of David and Goliath is a good example of that, isn't it?

Do you have any giant problems in your life? How do you think God would want you to face them?

[Have a good discussion with your child about his/her answers.]

I have "giants" in my own life—big problems that I have to face sometimes. Let's pray that God gives us the courage of David to face our problems. You pray about the giants in your life, and I'll pray about the ones in mine.

Dear God,
Thank You for David. He was a hero if there ever was one. His story makes me realize that when You are on our side, it doesn't make any difference who's on the other side, or how many enemies we face. Help us to stand up to the giants in our lives and not let them bully us the way Goliath bullied the Israelites. Thank You for giving us the courage of David. In Jesus' name we pray.
        Amen.

LET'S TALK ABOUT THE DAY
Good, Bad, or In-Between?

[This blessing includes meaningful touch. You might lightly brush your fingertips up and down your child's arm, or rub his/her back or shoulders, or smooth his/her hair. Choose the one most comfortable for you and your child.]

Let's talk about each other's day. While you talk, I'll lightly brush my fingertips up and down your arm *[or whatever form of touch you've chosen]*. When you're finished, I'll tell you about my day, and you can brush your fingertips up and down my arm. Okay?

So tell me. How was your day today? Was it a good day, a bad day, or just an in-between day?

[If the answer is good or bad, talk about it. What made it good? or, What made it bad? If the answer is in-between, ask your child, "What would have made the day a little better?"]

[Now change roles and let your child ask you about your day.]

Dear God,
Thank You for this day. Thank You for friends and family. Even though sometimes they drive us a little crazy, we love them, and we know they love us. Especially I thank you for _____ *[your child's name]*. What a wonderful gift he/she is to me.

     Amen.

LET'S LOOK IN THE BIBLE
Interruptions

[You will need a Bible.]

Tonight we're going to read a story about an interruption. Have you ever been interrupted when you've been doing something important or saying something important?

[Let your child respond.]

Sometimes interruptions can be irritating, can't they? But sometimes they can be important—as in this story.

[Read Luke 8:40–56.]

Jesus was on His way to do something important, wasn't He? What was it He was on His way to do?

Who interrupted Him? Was it important? How long had this woman been sick? How do you think she felt being sick all those years?

Because of the nature of her sickness, she couldn't go to worship at the synagogue, which is church for the Jewish people. And other people didn't associate with her because she was "unclean" from her sickness. She wouldn't get invited to parties or to weddings or to holiday gatherings. How do you think she felt about being excluded from those things?

Have you ever been excluded from something, like a game or a party? How did you feel? Imagine feeling that way for 12 years. That's how long this woman was excluded.

What did Jesus do to help her feel included?

[He healed her, but He also stopped, called her "daughter," and told the whole crowd that she was healed and that it was her faith that helped make her well again.]

How do you think that made her feel? How do you think it made the people in the crowd think about her?

Jesus set an example for us to follow. He asked us to treat others as we want to be treated. Let's ask God to help us do that each day.

Dear God,
It doesn't feel good to be on the outside. Help us realize that and not ever make someone feel left out. Help us to include other people in our meals, our games, our parties, even our conversations. Thank You for including us in Your family. We love You.
     Amen.

LET'S PLANT A SEED
The Golden Rule

[You will need an index card and something to write with.]

Let's plant another seed of truth in your heart. Pretty soon you're going to have a wonderful garden growing there. That's exciting! I can't wait to see what grows from these seeds, can you?

This verse is found in the Sermon on the Mount, which is the longest sermon we have recorded in the Bible, and the most beautiful.

"Do to others what you would have them do to you" (Matthew 7:12).

Let's first write the verse on this index card so you will be able to refresh your memory during the week. When you see the card, you can remember to think about the verse and pray about it.

[After you or your child has written the verse on the index card, discuss it.]

Do you know what this verse is called? It's called the Golden Rule. Why do you think people call it that?

[To illustrate the value of gold, you could use an example from the Olympics, with the bronze medal for third place,

the silver medal for second place, and the gold medal for first place.]

What do you think the verse means? Can you give an example to show what it means? Let's say, for instance, a friend of yours asks to be included in a game; how should you respond, according to this verse?

Now let's read the Golden Rule once together and then memorize it.

[Go over it several times, and include the reference as part of the memorization.]

Good job. Now let's put the index card in a place where you'll see it every day. Where would that be?

[Find the spot and leave the card there.]

Let's pray together, asking God to help us remember to treat people the way He wants us to. You start, and I'll finish.

Dear God,
Thank You for all the precious truths in Your Word. Surely this is one of the most precious, so precious we can truly call it golden. Help us never to forget it, and always to apply it. In Jesus' name we pray.
       Amen.

LET'S PLAY A GAME
Slapjack

[You will need a deck of cards. If you prefer to use "Old Maid" cards or "Go Fish" cards or others, just designate the cards to be slapped. Choose no more than four per deck.]

Let's play the game Slapjack. Here's how it's played. We put the deck between us, right in the middle, like this. Then we alternate being the dealer—the one who takes the cards off the top of the deck and turns them over. If you're the dealer, you can't look at the card. You have to just turn it over and put it down as fast as you can. If the card isn't a jack, you keep turning cards over, the faster the more fun.

If a jack comes up, the first one to slap it gets it and all the cards beneath it. The one who ends up with the most cards wins.

You have to be quick, but if you're too quick and slap a card that isn't a jack, you must give the other person one of your cards.

Any questions? Okay, I'll shuffle the cards, and we'll start.

[Have fun with your game. As you play, comment on times when your child shows quick responses.]

That was a fast-moving game, wasn't it? Let's quiet down now and talk to God together.

Dear God,
Help us realize that it's good to be observant, and often-times it's important to be quick, too. Your Word says we should be quick to listen. The Bible also tells us to be quick to obey and be quick to run away from anything that is bad or may be harmful to us. At the same time, Lord, help us realize that if we're too quick about some things, it might cause problems. In the same verse that tells us to be quick to listen, it also says to be "slow to speak and slow to become angry" (James 1:19). When it comes to our reactions, please help us make right choices in our lives. In Jesus' name we pray.
　　　　Amen.

LET'S BUILD SOMETHING
House of Cards

[You will need a Bible, a deck of cards, and two flat surfaces such as cutting boards.]

Tonight we're going to build a house—but not just any house. It's a house of cards. Here's how you do it.

[Demonstrate the process.]

The object of the game is to keep adding cards to your house until you're out of cards or until your house falls down. I'll divide the deck equally, and then we can start.

[Go through the building process until you both have something that remains standing. This may take several efforts. When both of you are done, read the story of the two men who each built a house—one on a solid foundation, the other on sand. The story comes at the end of the Sermon on the Mount in Matthew 7:24-27.]

[When you're finished reading, discuss the verse together. Then show your child how important it is to build a sturdy house. Use your own house as an example. Then contrast it to the house of cards. Show how fragile a card house is by letting your child take a card or a coin or a paper clip and throwing it at the house.]

Day by day, you and I are building a house with our lives. Which house would you rather have, our house or the house of cards? What do we have to do to build a sturdy house on a good foundation? What does Jesus say we have to do?

[Read Matthew 7:24.]

Dear God,
Help us to build our lives on the sturdy foundation of Your words. And help us to see that it's not enough just to hear the words. We have to act on them, obeying them and applying them to our lives. Watch over us as we build, and let us know if we're not doing it right. Thank You.

     Amen.

LET'S TALK ABOUT THE DAY
Things We Say

[As you talk with each other, provide some form of meaningful touch: brushing fingertips up and down the other person's arm, giving a back rub, or stroking the other person's hair. Choose a form of touch which is most comfortable for both of you.]

Let's talk about each other's day. While you talk, I'll lightly brush my fingertips up and down your arm *[or whatever form of touch you have chosen]*. When you're finished, I'll tell you about my day, and you can brush your fingertips up and down my arm *[or other choice]*. Okay?

So tell me. How was your day?

What was the nicest thing someone said to you today? How did you feel about that?

What was the meanest thing someone said to you? How did you feel about that?

Did you think about God today? If so, what were your thoughts?

Did you talk with God today? If so, what did you talk about?

Okay. Now let's trade places, and you ask me.

[When your conversation is finished, move into prayer time.]

It's nice to talk comfortably together, isn't it? Think how much God enjoys our conversations with Him, too. Let's spend some time thanking Him now.

Dear Lord,
Your Word says that Your compassions toward us are new every morning. Every morning! That's a great reason to go to bed, so that we might wake up to a new morning and find all the wonderful gifts You want to give us. Until tomorrow, give us good rest and sweet dreams. In Jesus' name we pray.
　　　Amen.

LET'S DO A FEW RIDDLES
Fast and Fun Ones

Here are a few riddles to get you thinking. Listen carefully. They're tricky.

[You'll find the answers on page 199.]

1. Which is worth more, an old five-dollar bill or a new one?

2. What animal took the most luggage on the ark?

3. What is the smallest bridge in the world?

4. When is a sheep like ink?

5. When is a door not a door?

6. What has teeth but never eats?

7. What is it that no one has ever seen, that never was, but always is to be?

8. What marches on, but has no feet?

9. What runs, but never gets tired?

10. How can you drop an egg three feet and have the egg not get broken?

Dear God,
Sometimes life seems so full of riddles—problems that don't have clear answers. When we can't figure one out, help us to remember the game we played tonight. Help us to understand that if we think about a life-question long enough, and if we ask You for wisdom, we'll often discover the answer. Thank You that You have the answer to every problem we face in life. In Jesus' name we pray.
Amen.

LET'S BE THANKFUL
Rubber Band Reminders

[You will need two rubber bands.]

[This blessing is designed for the night before Thanksgiving. If you wish to use it another time, you can adapt it to speak generally about giving thanks.]

The Bible talks a lot about being thankful. Paul tells us to give thanks to God in all circumstances (1 Thessalonians 5:18), especially when we're anxious (Philippians 4:6), and when we're singing spiritual songs (Colossians 3:16).

Can you think of some things you're thankful for?

Let's start by being thankful for who you are and how God made you.

Now tell me some things you're thankful for about home, and why.

Now tell me some people you're thankful for, and why.

Now tell me some things you're thankful for in nature.

And lastly, tell me some things about God that make you thankful.

You know that Thanksgiving is a holiday set aside each year to give thanks to God for all He has given us and how well He has taken care of us. Tomorrow we're going to celebrate Thanksgiving, but not with turkey and dressing and mashed potatoes. We're going to celebrate it by going through the day and being thankful for as much as we possibly can.

Here's a tool to help us remember to give thanks. I've got a rubber band for you and one for me. Put yours on tonight as a reminder, so when you wake up in the morning, you will remember to thank God. All through the day, whenever you notice the rubber band, stop what you're doing, look around you, and try to find something to be thankful for. Then tomorrow night we'll talk about it.

Dear God,
We have so much to be thankful for. Make us especially attentive tomorrow so we can notice all the wonderful things You have given us—things that not only feed us or protect us, but also make us happy.
     Amen.

LET'S TALK TOGETHER
Our Day of Thanksgiving

So, tell me, how did your day of thanksgiving go?

What did you give thanks to God for first? How about last? What were some of the things in the middle?

Was there something you saw that you had never given thanks for before?

What was the most unusual thing you gave thanks for?

How did you feel after a day of giving thanks?

How did it change you?

[Now you share how your day went, what you gave thanks for, and how it affected your attitude.]

Let's both pray tonight, and while we do, let's talk to God about some of the things we were thankful for today. You go first.

Thank You, God,
For little things, for thumbs and toes and the birds that sing. Thank You for big things, for sun and moon and especially spring. Thank You, too, for in-between things, for dogs and cats and backyard swings. Thank You for being so generous with us. We are grateful, so very, very grateful. Especially we thank You for giving us Your Son, the greatest gift of all. And it's in His name we pray.
      Amen.

LET'S PLAY A GAME
Helpful Hints

This is a game where one player thinks of a person, place, or thing. The other player asks questions to try to uncover what the first player is thinking of. The "thinker" should give helpful hints, answering the questions in a way that narrows the search.

Here's an example. Choose a category to begin. Let's say it's "plants."

Are you tall?

No, I am not a tree.

Are you short?

No, I am not grass.

Do you have petals?

Yes, but I am not a tulip.

Are you red?

No, I am not a rose.

Does your name have four syllables?

No, I am not a honeysuckle.

Does it have three syllables?

Yes, but I am not a carnation.

Are you a sunflower?

Yes.

[This game may be more difficult for younger children so you might want to pick a category that would be familiar to them.]

[When you are finished playing, ask your child if he or she would like to talk about any hard questions before going to sleep. Talk over the answers, and then turn to prayer time.]

Dear God,
Thank You for questions and for the fact that if we ask enough of them, eventually we will find an answer.
    Amen.

LET'S PRETEND
Fist Puppets

[You will need a pen or a washable marker.]

Make your hand into a fist. Good. Tonight we're going to pretend our fists can talk. But they can't talk without a mouth, and a mouth can't exist without a face, so we'll just have to draw one.

[Draw a face on the side of your child's fist, putting eyes near the lowest knuckle on the index finger, a nose under it, and lips all the way around the opening between your thumb and your finger. You've probably done this before or seen it done, but basically you move the thumb up and down to simulate talking. Draw one on your hand as well. If you want to be a little more authentic, put a small hat on the hand or a small wig. Also, you can use different colors for the face—blue for the eyes, brown for the hair, pinkish color for the lips.]

We can pretend our fist puppets are anyone or anything we want: a frog, a monkey, a dog, a cat, a person. You can even play with each other, go over a Bible memory verse, talk about the day, or sing a song. What do you want to be?

Now let's think of something to talk about.

[You can do some funny things with the character by putting your other thumb into the palm of your fisted hand and using it as you would a tongue, sticking it out of the mouth. Or you can close the mouth tightly, refusing to say anything.]

Dear God,
Thank You for the day today.
Thank You for the sun to greet and food to eat,
For a nice soft bed and a stomach that's fed,
For eyes to see and ears to hear,
We thank You, Lord, for all we hold dear.
      Amen.

LET'S PLAY A GAME
Beddy-bye

[You will need a few pieces of paper and a pencil.]

[This is a variation of the popular game known as Hangman.]

To start tonight's game, I'll ask you to draw a picture of a bed on this sheet of paper.

While you are drawing, I'll think of a word in my head. When I've got it, I'll draw blanks on your paper, one for every letter of the word. You have to guess a letter that might be part of the word. If you guess right, I'll put that letter in its proper place within the word. If there are two spaces for the letter you guess, I have to fill both of them.

If you guess a wrong letter, you have to start drawing a picture of yourself in bed. After 10 wrong guesses, you are complete, and it's bedtime.

[You can play for more than one game. You might go three rounds, for instance, so by the end of the third game, it would be bedtime.]

You start off with these parts and in this order:

1. The head, with eyes and a nose and a mouth

2. The body

3. One leg

4. The other leg

5. One arm

6. The other arm

7. One foot

8. The other foot

9. One hand

10. The other hand

Dear God,
Thank You for bedtime, even though it's hard to go to bed and say good-bye to the day and all the fun we are having. But if we don't go to bed, we can't wake up and greet a new day with the energy we need to live the day as fully as we can. So help _____ *[your child's name]* to fall asleep. And when we've both rested, help us to wake up with joyful hearts.

Amen.

LET'S TALK ABOUT THE DAY
What If . . .

This is a fun way to imagine. I'll ask you a "what if" question, and when you're finished answering it, you can ask me one. We'll go back and forth like that.

[Choose as few or as many of these conversation starters as you like.]

What if . . . you were king of the world?

[Your child's turn.]

What if . . . you were only four inches tall?

[Your child's turn.]

What if . . . everything you touched turned to chocolate?

[Your child's turn.]

What if . . . you had a time machine?

[Your child's turn.]

What if . . . you had a million dollars?

[Your child's turn.]

What if . . . you had three wishes that would come true?

[Your child's turn.]

What if . . . you could go to bed whenever you wanted?

[Your child's turn.]

What if . . . you got to go to heaven for a day and then came back to earth?

[Your child's turn.]

What if . . . you could talk with animals?

[Your child's turn.]

What if … one night it were Jesus who tucked you in bed?

[When you've had enough conversation, lead into the prayer time by saying something like the following.]

Did you have fun imagining how your life could be different? Now let's thank God for the life He has given you and for all the wonderful things in store that we can't even imagine!

Dear God,
Thank You for all You have given us and for all You will do for us in the future. Though it's fun to imagine different lives, we thank You for our lives right now, just the way they are. And if we were to change anything at all, we ask that You change us into people who are a little more patient, a little more kind, and a little more considerate of each other. That would be good.
Amen.

LET'S TALK ABOUT THE DAY
Happy or Sad?

[Before you begin this blessing, decide on a form of meaningful touch that you can give your child. Some ideas include:

- *Lightly brush your fingertips up and down your child's arm;*

- *Rub your child's back or shoulders;*

- *Smooth your child's hair.]*

So tell me. How was your day?

If you had the day to live over again, what would you change about it?

Did anything make you especially happy today?

Did anything make you a little sad?

Okay. Now you can ask me about my day. Either ask the questions I asked you, or come up with your own questions.

[Enjoy this time of sharing with your child.]

Now let's pray. Why don't you pray for some of the things I talked about in my day, and I'll pray for some of the things you talked about in yours. I'll go first this time, and when I'm finished, you can pray.

Dear God,
I thank You for today. It was a real gift. I would like to talk with You tonight about _____'s *[your child's name]* day. Especially I pray _____ *[use the specifics your child talked about to finish your prayer].* Goodnight, God. And we look forward to what awaits us tomorrow.

      Amen.

LET'S LEARN SOMETHING
The Redwood Tree

Do you know what the largest tree in the world is? It's the sequoia, commonly called the redwood tree. Most redwoods grow on the West Coast in northern California in a place called the Redwood National Forest. Some of the trees there are 3,000 years old. That's a thousand years before Jesus' time.

Some of the trees there grow to be nearly 300 feet tall. That's the length of a football field. So if you stood a football field on its end, that would be how tall some of those trees are.

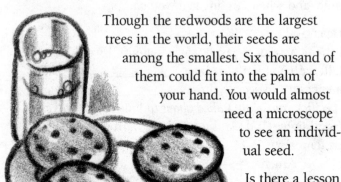

Though the redwoods are the largest trees in the world, their seeds are among the smallest. Six thousand of them could fit into the palm of your hand. You would almost need a microscope to see an individual seed.

Is there a lesson we can learn about life from the redwood tree?

One of the things God might teach us through its example is that great things often come from small beginnings. For instance, the whole nation of Israel began with one seed, Isaac, the child of Abraham and Sarah (Genesis 15:1-5). And God said that He would multiply that seed so that it would be as great in number as the sand on the seashore (Genesis 32:12). That's a lot, isn't it?

God likes to work through small things. A kind word. A smile. A hug. What are some other small things God uses that have huge results?

How about small children?

Dear God,
Thank You for using small things to produce great results. Just as a whole forest can grow from a tiny seed, so a great number of Christians may come from a small seed of kindness we plant in one person's life. Thank You that even small children like _____ *[your child's name]* can have a great effect upon the world.

    Amen.

LET'S PLAY A GAME
Checkers

[You will need a checkerboard and checkers. If you don't have one, look for one at a garage sale, or buy a simple, inexpensive game at a toy store.]

[Tonight teach your child how to play checkers. Even small children can learn in a short period of time. After you've explained the object of the game and the rules, play a game together. Your child will probably want to play again, but you can leave the box of checkers in the child's room and promise to play another day.]

[Playing a game like checkers provides an excellent opportunity to help your child develop a good attitude about winning and losing. Highly competitive children may take a while to learn good sportsmanship. Try discussing the following questions if your child is an especially poor loser when you play games together.]

142

How do you feel about losing?

Would the game be as much fun if you knew you would always win?

How do you think the winner feels when you complain about losing?

What could you do instead?

Dear God,
Thank You for _____ *[your child's name]*. I pray that he/she grows up to be strong, not just in body but in spirit. Watch over him/her and protect him/her as he/she grows. I can't wait to see what wonderful things You are going to do through _____'s *[your child's name]* life. In Jesus' name I ask this.
     Amen.

LET'S MAKE SOME LISTS
All About You and Me

[You will need several index cards and two pencils.]

Tonight we're going to make lists—as many as we want. Each list has to have 10 things on it, and each will focus on a different topic.

You can come up with your own ideas for the topics, but here are a few if you want some ideas to get started. We'll each arrange the items on our lists in order, from most to least.

[This may seem like a silly exercise, but it will help you learn about your child's likes and dislikes. Knowing these things can help you be a better parent as you understand your child more completely.]

1. Ten things I like for breakfast

2. Ten things I like for lunch

3. Ten things I like for dinner

4. Ten things that irritate me

5. Ten things that make me happy

6. Ten things I like to do

7. Ten things I don't like to do

8. Ten things I like about *[pick a person, teacher, pastor, parent, or friend]*

9. Ten things I don't like about being a child

10. Ten things I do like about being a child

11. Ten places I would like to go

12. Ten games I like to play

13. Ten rules I think are fair

14. Ten rules I think are unfair

[When the lists are finished, ask if you can have the cards, so you might have a better understanding of your child and so he or she might have a better understanding of you.]

Dear Lord,
Thank You for _____'s *[your child's name]* lists. Help me to use them to make me more sensitive to his/her needs and desires. Hopefully we will be able to talk about them, especially the dislikes, so we can understand each other better.

    Amen.

LET'S PLAY A GAME
Thumb Wrestling

Tonight we're going to wrestle, but we're going to do it with our thumbs. Have you ever done that before? Here's how we play. We sit opposite each other. You take your right hand, curling your fingers toward your palm, using only them to grab my fingers, which are also cupped.

Good. That's it. Then we rest our thumbs beside each other. When we count to start the game, we move our thumbs back and forth over and under each other. Try it.

Here's how we count together before we start:

"One, two, three, four.
Let's have a thumb war."

The object of the game is to wrestle your opponent's thumb and trap it for three seconds. If you do, you win.

Let's do a practice round or two, and then we'll play for real.

[You can play a number of times before calling it a night.]

Okay, my thumb is just too tired to go another round. Put your thumbs together, this time to pray. Why don't I start and you finish?

Dear God,
Thank You for our thumbs. Who ever thought they could be so much fun? Of course, they wouldn't be as much fun without another thumb to play with. Thank You that the other thumb belongs to my *[son or daughter]*, whom I love greatly. In Jesus' name we pray.
    Amen.

Let's Sing a Song
Oh, How I Love Jesus

Let's sing a song tonight. It's short, and it goes like this:

Oh, how I love Jesus,
Oh, how I love Jesus,
Oh, how I love Jesus,
Because He first loved me.

Did you know that song comes from a verse in the Bible?
The verse says: "We love because he first loved us"
(1 John 4:19).

That's a pretty good reason to love, isn't it? It's the same reason you love me. You love me for many reasons but the biggest reason is because I loved you first. I loved you before you had a name, before you were even born, before you could see me or understand me. I loved you before you could say my name. Before you could hug back or love back.

That's the way Jesus loved us. And that is why it is so easy to love Him back. Let's sing that song again.

Oh, how I love Jesus,
Oh, how I love Jesus,
Oh, how I love Jesus,
Because He first loved us.

Thank You, Jesus,
For loving us first, loving us best, and loving us forever. The more we find out about You—the more we discover how much You love us and sacrificed for us—the more we just naturally love You back. Thank You so much, so very, very much. We love You.
    Amen.

LET'S DO SOMETHING FUN
Banana Bash

[You will need two bananas that are without bruises or discolorations, and two straight pins.]

You probably know that fruit is good for you, but did you know it also can be fun?

Take these bananas, for instance. You can peel them and eat them, but you can play with them, too. Let me show you how. Take a pin and scratch the surface of the peel. Look what happens.

[The scratch will almost immediately start to turn brown.]

Now look.

[Write your name on the peel with the straight pin.]

What does it say?

Now you try. Take the banana in your hand and write something or draw something.

You can also use the pin to prick the banana peel in several places, and the pinpricks will turn dark.

[Demonstrate.]

Let's tattoo the whole banana, top to bottom.

[When the two of you are done, you can either eat your bananas or put them on display.]

Well, that was fun. Now let's get serious for a minute before we pray. What are some things on your heart—problems that you worry about—that you would like to pray about?

[You may need to ask several questions to help your child specify prayer requests.]

These are some of the things on my heart.

[Share prayer requests with your child.]

I'll tell you what. Why don't you pray for my things and I'll pray for yours? Do you want to start, or would you like me to begin?

Dear God,
I lift _____ *[your child's name]* up to You tonight. He/she has some things on his/her heart that are getting a little heavy, and we ask that You carry them. I pray _____ *[go through the various things your child wanted prayer for]*. We are grateful that You hear and that You care and that You always want to know what's going on in our lives. Thanks for listening.
Love, _____ *[your child's name]* and _____
[your name].

LET'S PLAY A GAME
Lightning Rounds

[You will need a watch or clock with a second hand, along with a pencil and paper.]

This game is called Lightning Rounds, because it is played as fast as lightning. The object of the game is to be the one to get the most words in one minute.

One person gives the other a letter, and that person then has one minute to name as many things beginning with that letter as possible.

Let's say, for example, I give you the letter B. I say "go," and you name as many words as you can that start with the letter B. I'll write them down as a way of keeping score. Ready to try it? Go.

[Some sample words might include: bee, beetle, boat, body, brain, big, black, blue, and so on.]

Do you understand? Okay. Let's play for real.

[Decide how many rounds you will play at the start of the game. After you are finished, tally the scores and see who has won.]

That game moved really fast, didn't it? We both had to think quickly, and the pressure was on. Do you think this game was a little like our real lives? We can find ourselves under pressure when we have a lot to do and not much time to do it. I know God can help us with that. Let's talk to Him now, okay?

Dear God,
It's hard to think when everything is going so fast—in a game and in real life, too. Teach us that faster is not always better. Help us to slow down and enjoy the words that other people say. Help us to make right choices, even when the pressure is on. Thank You for the fun we had tonight. We'll see You in the morning.

Love, _____ [your child's name] and _____ [your name].

LET'S PLAN A PROJECT
Cookie Choices

[You will need a cookbook with a cookie section, an index card, and a pencil.]

I'm getting hungry for some homemade cookies. How about you?

Tonight we can look through this cookbook together, pick out the cookies we would like to make, and list the ingredients we don't have. Tomorrow I'll go to the store and get them, and about 30 minutes before bedtime we'll bake a batch and then enjoy our cookies and milk.

What do you think about that?

[Sit beside your child and slowly page through the cookbook. Talk over the possibilities, but let the final decision be your child's. Once a cookie recipe has been picked, read the list of ingredients. If you don't have all the ingredients, use the index card to list those you need. Now read the instructions. If you want, you may comment on some of the ingredients or the instructions. Make this a good learning experience for your child.]

Well, that's something to look forward to, isn't it? They're going to be so-o-o-o yummy in our tummy. I can't wait.

But we'll have to. As hard as it is to
wait, waiting is often good for us.
It teaches us to be patient, and
that's a good thing, isn't it? It's
one kind of fruit the Holy Spirit
produces in our lives; did you
know that? Let's talk to
God about helping us
wait patiently.

Dear God,
We thank You already
for tomorrow. We
don't know what all
tomorrow holds, but
we know one thing it
holds: cookies. And though we can't wait, we'll have to.
Teach us to be patient in the waiting. We love You.

From _____ *[your child's name]* and _____
[your name].
        Amen.

LET'S MAKE SOMETHING
Cookies!

[You will need to make the cookies with your child at least 30 minutes before bedtime. Bring a plate of them and two glasses of milk to your child's bedroom. Be sure to bring the cookbook you used.]

Yummy! These are great, aren't they?

[For a few minutes just enjoy the cookies and milk and each other, then bring out the cookbook and turn to your cookie recipe. Read the ingredients out loud again.]

Did you think it would take all those ingredients to make a simple cookie? What if we didn't have all the ingredients, but we were so hungry we didn't care and made the cookies anyway?

Let's say we didn't have flour. What do you think that would have done to the cookies? Or maybe we were all out of butter *[or oil]*. How do you think the cookies would taste? But imagine we were so hungry, nothing could stop us. How enjoyable would it be to eat those cookies? Instead of "yummy," we'd be saying "yucky," wouldn't we?

A lot of ingredients go into a life to make a person—a good person, that is. If you had to come up with a recipe to make a good person, what ingredients would you list? Why those? Are you missing anything? We don't want to make a yucky person, do we?

Good. Let's pray that God gives us all the ingredients we need—and in just the right measure—so our lives will smell as good and taste as good as these cookies.

Will you lead the prayer tonight? And don't forget to thank God for the cookies!

[Let your child pray.]

LET'S TALK ABOUT SOMETHING
Hurting Words

There's a saying that goes like this: "Sticks and stones may break my bones, but words will never hurt me." Often that saying is used as a reply to someone who is making fun of us. It comes in handy sometimes, but is it true?

Will words never hurt us? What do you think?

Can you remember a time when someone hurt you with words?

I remember a time when I was hurt by somebody's words.

[Share an experience from your life.]

Why do you think words hurt so much?

Can you think of a time when your words hurt someone else? How did you feel about it afterward?

I remember a time I hurt someone with my words.

[Describe the experience.]

Words can cause a wound, or they can heal a wound. It's amazing the power that words have, isn't it?

The Bible says we should be careful with our words. Life and death are in the power of the tongue—in other words, our speech (see Proverbs 18:21). James warns us that the tongue is something that is hard to control, and when it gets out of control (like when you yell at someone in anger), it can be as destructive as fire (James 3:2-8).

Let's pray about how we use our words, okay? You go first, then I'll follow.

Dear Lord,
The tongue does seem like a small fire, and it can get out of control before we know it. People can either be warmed by our words or burned by them. Please help me to be careful about what I say. Help _____
[your child's name], too. And if we forget, please remind and correct us.
        Amen.

LET'S MAKE SOMETHING
Favorite Things Poster

[You will need a large piece of poster board, a felt marker, and tape or thumbtacks.]

There's a wonderful movie and stage musical called *The Sound of Music,* which is based on the story of a real person. Maria is a brave young woman who becomes a nanny to the seven children of Captain von Trapp. They live on a large estate in Austria, and Maria must help the children learn and grow in many ways.

Maria uses songs to teach the children, songs she learned as a nun in a nearby abbey. One night, when there is a frightening storm, she helps the children overcome their fears by thinking happy thoughts. They sing the song "My Favorite Things."

Favorite things are important, not just because they give us joy, but because they tell us a lot about who we are. Tonight let's list some of your favorites on this poster.

Favorite dessert: _____.

Favorite song: _____.

Favorite game: _____.

Favorite movie: _____.

Favorite book: _____.

Favorite color: _____.

Favorite holiday: _____.

Favorite animal: _____.

Favorite memory: _____.

Favorite season: _____.

Favorite TV show: _____.

Favorite verse in the Bible: _____.

Favorite nighttime activity that we've done: _____.

Now that we're finished, we're going to put the poster up on the wall. When you look at the poster, think about these favorite things and what they mean to you. Some of these things tell us a lot about the special person that you are. It's good to be reminded of that.

[Challenge your child to think about what this list says about him/her as a person. Let him/her know that you'll be talking more about this tomorrow night.]

Now let's talk to God together.

Dear God,
Thank You for all of _____'s *[your child's name]* favorite things. You are teaching him/her so many new things, about the world and about himself/herself. Please help _____ *[your child's name]* continue to grow into a person who loves and honors You. In Jesus' name we pray.
    Amen.

LET'S TALK TOGETHER
Your Favorite Things and You

Did you have some time to think about some of your favorite things on this poster? What do you think they say about you?

For example, your favorite season is _____. Why? What is so special about that season to you?

[You may discover the preference is based on activities that happen, or don't happen, during that season: no school in summer; sports in the fall; Christmas in winter, etc.]

What does your choice tell us about you—a special and unique individual?

[Go through your child's entire favorite things poster, asking questions similar to those above, and see what the answers reveal about his/her personality, attitudes, and preferences.]

Father,
Thank You for what we learned tonight. I enjoyed discovering more about _____ *[your child's name]*. He/she is a pretty terrific kid. But, of course, You know that. I hope he/she knows it, too.

Amen.

LET'S BE THANKFUL
Thank You for Parents

The apostle Paul tells us to be thankful in everything.

What are you thankful for?

Have you ever thought of being thankful for the things your parents do for you? For example, think about some of the things your parents say that you are thankful for.

[Have your child list several before stopping.]

Now think about some of the things your parents *do* that you are thankful for.

[Again, have your child list several things.]

Tonight I'm going to ask you to pray, so you can tell God some of those things you are thankful for. Remember that sometimes we place our hands on the person we are praying for, as a special way of blessing and encouraging him or her. Tonight, as you pray, why don't you put your hand on my shoulder or arm? That would be a special blessing for me.

[Now your child prays his or her prayer.]

LET'S DO SOMETHING
Mailing You to Someone Special

[This one is going to take a little more work on your part, but trust me, it will be worth it. You will need some white butcher paper. Since butchers don't use it much anymore, you may have to visit an office products store or art supply shop. Or try a print shop to see if they have any end rolls of paper. You will need a mailing tube that is a little longer than the height of the butcher paper. You will also need a variety of either felt markers or crayons.]

Tonight we're going to get you ready to send through the mail.

[Spread the butcher paper out a little longer than your child is tall.]

We're not really going to send you. We're going to send a picture of you. Lie down on the paper, and I'll trace you.

[A washable felt marker will be easiest to work with.]

Okay. Now my part is done. Stand up and look. Pretty good resemblance, don't you think? Your job is to fill in the details. You'll need to draw your face and clothes by yourself. While you are doing this, be thinking of someone special you might want to send it to.

[When the figure is finished, have your child autograph it, date it, and write his or her age.]

Who did you decide on? Good. Now let's put a personal note with it, roll it up, and put it in the mailing tube. Tomorrow I'll send it in the mail. This is going to be a great gift!

Thank You, Lord,
For my child who, from the looks of the picture, is growing up fast. Help me not to miss a moment, because each second with _____ *[your child's name]* is so precious to me. I'll treasure these times with him/her for the rest of my life.
  Amen.

LET'S FIND OUT
"Why?" Questions

"Why" is a wonderful word. Do you want to know why? Because it helps us explore the world around us. "Why" is like a key that unlocks a lot of doors, revealing what is inside.

Let's ask a few "whys" and see what we discover.

Why do you think baby teeth fall out?

Here's why. Because children are so small, you need teeth that fit the small size of your mouth. These are called baby teeth. As you get bigger, your mouth gets bigger, too, and pretty soon the baby teeth no longer fit. When a permanent tooth is ready to come in, it releases a chemical that dissolves the roots of the tooth it is trying to replace. That is why the tooth starts to feel loose. Its roots are starting to dissolve.

Do you have a "why" question?

[Allow your child to think awhile to come up with a question. Then do your best to answer it.]

Why do you think you yawn when you get sleepy?

When the oxygen supply to your brain decreases, you start getting sleepy. When the oxygen supply gets low,

your brain triggers a response to help it
get more oxygen. That is why a yawn
happens. Your brain has sent a signal
to your body that it is not getting
enough oxygen, and your body
responds with a yawn that
draws in extra air.

Do you have another "why" question?

*[Continue your talk until you run out of
questions, answers, or time.]*

Dear God,
There are a lot of "whys" in the Bible. Some of them lead
to answers; some of them don't. Thank You for creating
us to be curious, and for such a wide and wonderful
world to be curious about. It's fun discovering things.
We'll talk to You in the morning.

Love, _____ *[your child's name]* and _____
[your name].

LET'S READ A BOOK
Classic Stories

[You will need to buy or get from the library a picture book or short book which is age-appropriate for your child. You may have to start bedtime a half-hour to an hour earlier to allow enough time to read the story aloud.]

[Let me suggest the following classic children's books:

The Giving Tree *by Shel Silverstein*

The Velveteen Rabbit *by Marjorie Williams*

The Fairy Tales of Grimm, *illustrated by Arthur Rackham*

Fairy Tales *by Hans Christian Andersen*

Aesop's Fables, *a version with good illustrations and a readable text for your child's age*

The Happy Prince and Other Fairy Tales *by Oscar Wilde*

Where the Wild Things Are *by Maurice Sendak. (This story could be compared to the parable of the prodigal son.)*

Any of the Winnie the Pooh *books by A. A. Milne*

Any of the Frog and Toad *books by Arnold Lobel*

Any of the Dr. Seuss books]

[Almost all children love to be read to. Cuddle up next to your child and have a great time reading together. Talk about the story when you are finished.]

Dear Father,
Thank You for all the wonderful stories that there are in the world and for all the people who wrote them. Especially we thank You for tonight's story and the fun we had reading it together.

Amen.

LET'S PRETEND
If I Were an Animal

Sometimes we can learn by pretending to be someone or something else. It's make-believe, of course, but let's try it. Let's pretend that we're animals, and that we can see the world through the animals' eyes.

Choose an animal and tell me what you see and what you learn from what you see.

[You might need to ask your child some questions to help lead your imaginations and the conversation that follows. Questions could include:

- *What do you use for shelter?*
- *What do you eat?*
- *How do you get your food?*
- *When and where do you sleep?*
- *Do you have a family? What is it like?*
- *How do you react to people?*
- *How do people treat you?*
- *Are you ever afraid?*
- *What can you do to protect yourself?*
- *What's the best thing about being the animal you are?*
- *How does the world seem different from your new point of view?]*

[After your child is finished, you choose an animal and play the pretending game.]

[When you are finished, explain that when we practice looking at the world from another view-point, we learn to deal with people who may be very different from us. This is an important skill. God has created each of us in a special way, and since we are not all alike, we have to work at understanding each other.]

Let's keep working on seeing the world from others' points of view. It's a gift God gives us to help us show love and concern for other people. Shall we talk with Him about that right now?

Dear God,
Help us to see the world as other people see it. This is the beginning of compassion, because we gain a new understanding about people. Teach us, O God. Change us. Help us to keep growing to be like Your Son.
Amen.

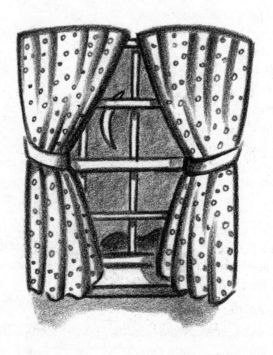

LET'S WRITE A POEM
Name Acrostic

[You will need a pencil and paper.]

Let's write a poem. In our poem, each line is going to start with a letter that spells the name of one of your friends. Which friend's name should we use?

[Write that child's name vertically on a piece of paper.]

Let's think of something you like about that friend that starts with the first letter of his/her name. It can be one word or a few words.

[Help your child think of words and fill in the acrostic. Don't worry about making the lines similar to each other. This poem is about friendship, not perfect poetry. Help your child decide what a good friend is like.]

[Read the poem aloud, then pray.]

Dear God,
You have made _____ *[name of your child's friend]* such a special person. Thank you that he/she is a good friend to _____ *[your child's name]*. Help him/her be a good friend to _____ *[name of your child's friend]*.
      Amen.

LET'S LOOK IN THE BIBLE
What Is Love?

[You will need a Bible and a dictionary.]

Tonight we're going to look up an important word. Maybe it's the most important word in the whole universe. What do you think that might be?

It's the word "love." Let's look it up in a dictionary and see how love is defined.

[Look up the word. My dictionary says love is "a strong affection or attachment or devotion to a person or persons."]

That doesn't sound like a very good definition of one of the greatest, if not the greatest word in the whole universe, does it?

Let's look in the Bible and see if we can find a better one.

[Read 1 Corinthians 13:4-5.]

That tells us more about love than the dictionary does, doesn't it? Does this mean if we're impatient with each other, we're not being loving? Does it mean if we're unkind to each other, we're not loving each other?

Let's look at some more verses.

[Read 1 John 4:7-21.]

That passage has a lot to say about love, doesn't it? I especially like verse 20.

[Read it again.]

What do you think that means?

[Read 1 John 5:3.]

What does that verse tell us about love? Now let's turn to another verse.

[Read Galatians 5:22a: "The fruit of the Spirit is love."]

Why do you think it says that love is a fruit? Who produces this fruit in us?

The Bible sure has a lot to say about love, doesn't it? It tells us so much more than the dictionary. Let's pray now and ask God to help us to be more loving to each other.

Dear God,
We just read that You are love. What a wonderful definition. Help us to love others the way You do. Help us to be patient with them, kind to them, and whenever they might be ugly to us or say mean things, help us not to make a list of those wrongs and carry a grudge. Help us to forgive them instead, because You are love, and that is what You would do. In Jesus' name we pray.
      Amen.

LET'S TALK ABOUT CHOICES
What Would You Do?

We all have to make choices in life. Some are easy—such as which cereal you choose in the morning. Some are more difficult—like the ones we're going to talk about tonight. I'll give you a difficult situation, and you tell me what choice you would make.

Situation #1
Your parents have let you sit with a friend in church. You are sitting there quietly, trying to listen to the pastor. Your friend isn't paying attention and wants you to play tic-tac-toe on the church bulletin. Your parents don't like you doing that in church, but they won't see you doing it. Will you do it? Why?

Situation #2
Someone has left a pocketful of change on the kitchen counter. It looks like as much as a dollar in coins. The money has been sitting on the counter for three days. If you take a dime, it's likely no one will notice. Will you take the money? Why?

Situation #3

Some kids in the neighborhood—kids you know well—are making fun of a younger kid that you don't know well. You are there while this is going on. What will you do? Why?

[You may want to read several Bible verses that shed light on the choices we should be making in our lives. These might include: Ephesians 6:1-3, Ephesians 4:28, Ephesians 4:29.]

Dear God,

It's not always easy to do the right thing, but whenever we do, we know that Your way is best for us and those around us. Most of all, we know that when we act the way You want, You are pleased. Help us to make the right choices, even when those choices are hard. After all, that's what Jesus did. It's in His name we pray.

Amen.

LET'S PLAY A GAME
Nim

[You will need a couple of colored pens or pencils and a piece of paper.]

The game we're going to play tonight is a very, very old game. It is called Nim. Here is the most popular version, though there are a number of variations.

Draw 15 lines like the ones below:

Top row

| | | | | |

Middle row

| | | | |

Bottom row

| | |

You can start on any row and cross out as many lines as you like, but you must stay on that row. When you're finished, I pick a row and cross out as many lines as I like. It could be the same row you picked, or I could pick another line. And we go back and forth like that. To win, you can't be the one who crosses out the last line.

Here's an example of how the game is played:

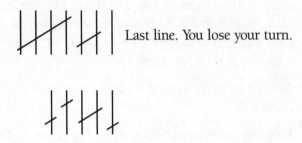

Last line. You lose your turn.

Dear God,
Thank You for today. Thank You for the sun that warmed us and the food that nourished us. Thank You for the hugs that warmed us, too, in a different way from the sun, but just as real and just as important. Thank You, too, for Your Word, which is food for our souls, and nourishes us in ways that earthly food can never do.

      Amen.

LET'S LOOK IN THE BIBLE
New Rules

[You will need a Bible.]

[While you go through this evening's activity, go to the foot of the bed and massage your child's feet. Our feet are under more stress than any other part of the body, but we don't often realize it until someone rubs them. While you rub, talk to your child about rules.]

Tonight we're going to talk about rules. How do you feel about rules?

Rules are necessary to keep order. For example, they help with traffic. Imagine what it would be like if there were no rules about driving. No speed limits. No stop signs. No lines to mark off lanes. No traffic lights. Before very long, what would happen?

The same thing could happen to our lives. Our lives could turn into a traffic jam or a real bad wreck if it weren't for rules. That's why rules are necessary. They guide us safely through life.

If you were elected Rule-maker of the Universe, what 10 rules would you make? They can be rules for the house, rules for children, rules for adults, rules for eating, anything you want. After all, you are Rule-maker of the Universe. For tonight, anyway.

[When your child has finished, turn to Exodus 20:1-17.]

Would you like to know what rules that the real Ruler of the Universe has given for us to follow? They're called the Ten Commandments.

[Now read them.]

Think about these rules, and tomorrow night we'll talk about them.

Dear God,
Thank You that You are a God of order, both in the physical world and in the spiritual world. Thank You for the rules You have given us that help us to travel safely through this world of ours. Where would we be without You?

Amen.

LET'S LOOK IN THE BIBLE
The Ten Commandments

[You will need your Bible.]

Let's read the Ten Commandments again to refresh our memories about what we read last night.

[Read Exodus 20:1-17.]

[Next, set your Bible down and start rubbing your child's feet again, as you did last night. Talk about the questions which follow.]

What do you think about God's rules?

Do you have questions about any of them?

[You should probably brush up on terms such as "the Sabbath" and "covet" and "honor." Help your child understand the meaning of the commandments.]

Which one of these rules do you have the most difficult time obeying? Why?

Let me stop rubbing your feet now, and we'll look in the Bible to see just how important these feet of yours are.

Watch the path of your feet,
And all your ways will be established.
Do not turn to the right nor to the left;
Turn your foot from evil.
(Proverbs 4:26-27, NASB)

Why don't you pray tonight? Especially pray that your
feet stay on the path which God has designed for them.

[Let your child say tonight's prayer.]

LET'S PLAY A GAME
Non-stop Talk

[You will need a timer or a watch with a second hand.]

Here's the game for tonight. We're going to see if we can talk on a subject for three minutes without stopping. We can pause to take a breath, but no longer than five seconds. If we go over that, we lose.

That probably wouldn't be so hard, but the one who picks the topic is your opponent. The topics can be anything: trees, cooking, cleaning, animals, stories.

Why don't I take the first turn as a trial run so you'll understand. You pick a topic.

[Once your child has picked the topic, hand over the watch, and start talking.]

Now let's play for real.

[Some other topics could be: a vacation, a day at the zoo, your most embarrassing moment, going to church.]

Whew! I don't know about you, but I'm about all talked out. But I still have enough words for our prayer tonight.

Dear God,
Who would ever have thought that talking would be such hard work? How difficult it must be for people in professions that require them to talk a lot. Like a school teacher. Or someone who trains soldiers. Or a salesperson. Thank You for the gift of being able to talk. I love to hear what _____ *[your child's name]* has to say. We're glad You want to listen to whatever we tell You, too.

      Amen.

LET'S READ
Your Story

[You will need a children's book whose main character is the same gender as your child.]

I'm going to read you a story tonight. But it's going to be a different kind of story. Do you know why?

Because the main character is going to be you. I'm going to drop you right into the story. And I'm going to leave you there until the story ends.

[Start reading. Every time the main character's name appears, substitute your child's name. Besides being fun, this will make your child feel really special.]

Now that we're done with the story, you can come out of the book and go back home. How did it feel to be the main character in a story?

Did you know you are the main character in a real-life story? It's your story. That's right. You have a story—the story of your life. And God is using you as the main character to tell it. Now how does that make you feel?

Dear God,
Thank You for the story You are telling through
_____'s [your child's name] life. Help him/her to be
strong and courageous, for there will be a lot of difficult
decisions that someday he/she will have to make. Until
then, give him/her a good night's sleep so he/she can be
strong for tomorrow. In Jesus' name we pray.

      Amen.

LET'S TALK ABOUT NATURE
Clouds

Clouds are beautiful, aren't they? How many different kinds of clouds have you seen?

Some clouds look like thin feathers that brush across the sky. Others are fluffy like big balls of cotton. Others look like thin streaks across the sky.

Some clouds are rain clouds, some are snow clouds, and some are just ordinary fair-weather clouds.

Have you ever looked at the clouds and watched them as they change shape? Do you know what causes them to change shape? The wind. It may not feel windy to you as you watch clouds change, because the wind that moves the clouds is high, high in the sky.

Have you ever looked at clouds and thought you've seen the shape of something familiar, like a dog or a face or a toy? I think it's fun to just lie on my back and watch clouds float by.

Do you know what clouds are made of? Clouds are really drops of water that float in the sky. A cloud is like a whole country of drops that are so small you can't see them.

Do you know where clouds go? They go wherever the wind takes them. Or sometimes they break up into smaller clouds. Still other clouds drop their water as rain and disappear.

The Bible says life is like a vapor or mist, which is what a cloud is made of (James 4:13-14).

[Talk with your child about the temporary nature of clouds. Explain how James is comparing that to the temporary nature of our lives. Remind your child that while our lives on earth may one day be over, we will live forever in heaven with Jesus if we trust Him and follow Him.]

Dear God,
Thank You for the clouds which bring rain and create lovely sky pictures. We know our earthly lives are like a cloud, a vapor that appears for a while and then disappears. While we are here, help us to make our lives beautiful, the way Jesus' life was beautiful. With Your help, we can make the most of every single day.
　　　Amen.

LET'S HAVE A RIDDLE
Can You Guess?

[Here are some riddles that will be fun for the two of you to solve. If you get stumped, the answers are on p. 200.]

1. What word is always spelled incorrectly?

2. What is black and white and read all over?

3. What is black and white and red all over?

4. What did the girl volcano say to the boy volcano?

5. Why did the boy take the ruler to bed?

6. What would you get if Batman and Robin got stampeded by a herd of elephants?

7. How can you jump off a 50-foot ladder without getting hurt?

8. A police officer had a brother, but the brother had no brother. How can this be?

9. What is a twip?

10. What did the blind man say when he got a comb for a gift?

That was a lot of fun, wasn't it? Now let's get serious for a moment. What would you like to pray about tonight?

Dear God,
Riddles are fun because they make us think and they make us laugh. Thank You for our minds and for the gift of shared laughter. I'm so glad _____ *[your child's name]* knows how to enjoy life. *[Pray for what your child shared with you.]*
    Amen.

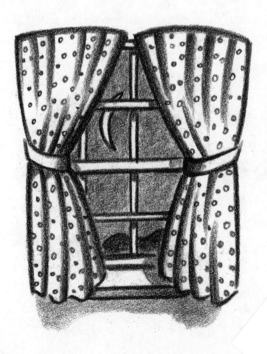

LET'S PRETEND
Touched by Jesus

[You will need a Bible.]

[Read Mark 10:13-16, the passage where Jesus blesses the children who are brought to Him. This is one of the great passages that talks about "the Blessing" and how it is imparted. Notice the words that affirm the children's future, the spoken blessing, and the physical touch.]

Let's pretend now, okay? Imagine you're one of the little children that Jesus gathered around Him and blessed.

How do you feel about the way He told off some of the adults and stood up for the children?

What do you imagine His eyes might look like? How about His face?

What words do you think He spoke when He blessed you and the other children?

What would you like to ask Jesus if He set you on His knee?

Based on this experience you had with Jesus, if someone were to ask you who Jesus was, what would you tell him?

Let's pray. Tonight I'll be the one who prays, okay?

[Gather your child in your arms as you pray.]

Dear Jesus,
Thank You for this dear child that I now hold in my arms. *[Now lay your hands on your child, say a blessing over your child's life, and affirm the special future that God has for your child.]*
  Amen.

LET'S LEARN A NEW WORD
Heaven

[You will need a Bible, an index card, and a pen or pencil.]

The new word for today is "Heaven." What do you think of when you think of heaven?

[Listen as your child expresses ideas about heaven. You may need to ask questions to help.]

Some people think heaven is a dull and drab place. They think that life on earth is the fuller experience and that life in heaven is the lesser experience. By that I mean some people think life on earth is in full color, yet life in heaven is only black and white. But the opposite is true.

In the movie *The Wizard of Oz*, life on earth is filmed in black and white. Life in Oz is shown in full color. The colors are brighter. The plants are bigger. The Emerald City is more beautiful than any city on earth. That is more what heaven is like. When Dorothy opened her door and walked into the land of Oz, she oohed and ahhed over everything she saw there.

That's what it will be like when we go to heaven. The apostle Paul was once given a glimpse of heaven. Here is what he saw:

[Read 2 Corinthians 12:2-4 and 1 Corinthians 2:9.]

Jesus talked about heaven, too. Right before His death, He said this:

[Read John 14:2-4.]

In light of those verses, what definition of heaven would you want to put on this index card?

[Have your child write the definition, but if your child can't write, you record his/her words. Then place the card in a prominent spot in the room.]

Dear Jesus,
Thank You that You went to heaven.
We're glad You are there now—preparing a place for us.
Whatever else heaven may be, we know it is the place
we will share with You forever. We can't wait to go, so
we can be with You there. Until we go, may we prepare
in our hearts a place for You.

     Amen.

LET'S SING A SONG
"Michael, Row the Boat Ashore"

Tonight's song is "Michael, Row the Boat Ashore." It's a restful song, and one we can harmonize on. Here's how it goes.

[You may want to sing it or just speak it.]

> Michael, row the boat ashore, Hallelujah
> Michael, row the boat ashore, Hallelujah
> My brothers and sisters are all aboard, Hallelujah
> My brothers and sisters are all aboard, Hallelujah
> Michael, row the boat ashore, Hallelujah
> Michael, row the boat ashore, Hallelujah
> The river is deep and the river is wide, Hallelujah
> Milk and honey on the other side, Hallelujah
> Michael, row the boat ashore, Hallelujah
> Michael, row the boat ashore, Hallelujah
> Jordan's river is chilly and cold, Hallelujah
> Chills the body but warms the soul, Hallelujah
> Michael, row the boat ashore, Hallelujah
> Michael, row the boat ashore, Hallelujah

Thank You, Lord.

Just like the song says, we will someday be rowed from the shores of this earth to the shores of heaven, a land of milk and honey, and a place where all our brothers and sisters in Christ will be. Until we get there and see You there, goodnight.

Amen.

Answer Page

Page 30—Let's Solve a Problem: The Envelope Puzzle

The solution to the envelope problem is this:

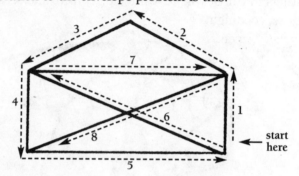

Page 80—Let's Have a Riddle: Quick Riddles

1. See you at the corner.

2. I've got you covered.

3. A potato.

4. An ear of corn.

5. A shoe.

6. A table.

7. A strand of hair.

8. Your name.

9. Heat, because you can catch a cold.

10. When you're in bed.

11. Twice. Once in the morning and once in the afternoon, when time lands on the exact hour and minute where the watch has stopped.

12. Your teeth.

13. Your nose.

14. Time.

15. A doorbell.

Page 124—Let's Do a Few Riddles: Fast and Fun Ones

1. An old five is worth four more dollars than a new one.

2. The elephant, because it took its trunk.

3. The bridge of your nose.

4. When it is in a pen.

5. When it's a jar.

6. A comb.

7. Tomorrow.

8. Time.

9. A clock.

10. Drop it from a height of four feet. For the first three feet, it won't break.

Page 190—Let's Have a Riddle: Can You Guess?

1. Incorrectly.

2. A newspaper.

3. A sunburned zebra.

4. Do you lava (love) me as much as I lava you?

5. To see how long he slept.

6. Flatman and Ribbon.

7. Jump off the bottom rung.

8. The officer was a woman.

9. A twip is what a wabbit takes when he wides a twain.

10. I'll never part with this.

About the Author

John Trent, president of Encouraging Words, holds a Ph.D in marriage and family counseling from Texas State University. He has written or co-authored more than a dozen books. He is an author and speaker for Focus on the Family's Heritage Builders ministry, which encourages parents to pass their faith to their children. If you would like to have John speak at your church, call Encouraging Words at 1-800-900-8640.

Welcome to the $\mathcal{F}$*amily!*

Heritage Builders

Helping You Build a Family of Faith

We hope you've enjoyed this book. Heritage Builders was founded in 1995
three fathers with a passion for the next generation. As a new ministry of
Focus on the Family, Heritage Builders strives to equip, train and motivate p
ents to become intentional about building a strong spiritual heritage.

It's quite a challenge for busy parents to find ways to build a spiritual
foundation for their families—especially in a way they enjoy and understan
Through activities and participation, children can learn biblical truth in
a way they can understand, enjoy—and *remember.*

Passing along a heritage of Christian faith to your family is a parent's highe
calling. Heritage Builders' goal is to encourage and empower you in this gre
mission with practical resources and inspiring ideas that really work—
and help your children develop a lasting love for God.

***

How To Reach Us

For more information, visit our Heritage Builders Web site! Log on to
www.heritagebuilders.com to discover new resources, sample activities
and ideas to help you pass on a spiritual heritage. To request any of thes
resources, simply call Focus on the Family at 1-800-A-FAMILY
(1-800-232-6459) or in Canada, call 1-800-661-9800. Or send
your request to Focus on the Family, Colorado Springs, CO 80995.
In Canada, write Focus on the Family, P.O. Box 9800,
Stn. Terminal, Vancouver, B.C. V6B 4G3

To learn more about Focus on the Family or to find out if there is an
associate office in your country, please visit www. family.org

We'd love to hear from you!

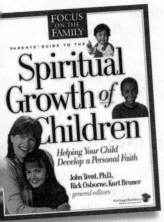

Mealtime Moments

Make your family's time around the dinner table meaningful with *Mealtime Moments,* a book that brings you great discussion starters an activities for teaching your children about your faith. Kids will have fu getting involved with games, trivia questions and theme nights, all base on spiritually sound ideas. Perfect for the whole family! Spiralbound.

Bible Stories for Preschoolers (New Testament) Family Nights Tool Chest

The ideas and activities you'll find in *Bible Stories for Preschoolers (New Testament)* are designed to make lasting impressions for the next generation. Part of the Heritage Builders "Family Nights Tool Chest" series, the paperback contains complete, clear plans to help kids learn spiritual truths from 13 of the most memorable stories from the New Testament.

• • •

Visit our Heritage Builders Web site! Log on to **www.heritagebuilders.com** to discover new resources, sample activities, and ideas to help you pass on a spiritual heritage. To request any of these resources, simply call Focus on the Family at 1-800-A-FAMILY (1-800-232-6459) or in Canada, call 1-800-661-9800 Or send your request to Focus on the Family, Colorado Springs, CO 80995. In Canada, write Focus on the Family, P.O. Box 9800, Stn. Terminal, Vancouver, B.C. V6B 4G3.

Heritage
Builders

Helping You Build a Family of Faith

Every family has a heritage—a spiritual, emotional, and social
legacy passed from one generation to the next. There are four
main areas we at Heritage Builders recommend parents consider
as they plan to pass their faith to their children:

Family Fragrance

Every family's home has a fragrance. Heritage Builders encourages parents to
create a home environment that fosters a sweet, Christ-centered AROMA
of love through Affection, Respect, Order, Merriment, and Affirmation.

Family Traditions

Whether you pass down stories, beliefs and/or customs, traditions can help
you establish a special identity for your family. Heritage Builders encourages
parents to set special "milestones" for their children to help guide them
and move them through their spiritual development.

Family Compass

Parents have the unique task of setting standards for normal,
healthy living through their attitudes, actions and beliefs. Heritage
Builders encourages parents to give their children the moral navigation
tools they need to succeed on the roads of life.

Family Moments

Creating special, teachable moments with his or her children is one of a parent's
most precious and, sometimes, most difficult responsibilities. Heritage Builders
encourages parents to capture little moments throughout the day to teach
and impress values, beliefs, and biblical principles onto their children.

We look forward to standing alongside you as you seek to impart the Lord's care
and wisdom to the next generation—to your children.

Heritage
Builders

Helping You Build a Family of Faith

11/02